Y0-ABH-108

WITHDRAWN
UTSA LIBRARIES

NOBLE NUMBERS,
SUBTLE WORDS

NOBLE NUMBERS, SUBTLE WORDS

The Art of Mathematics
in the Science of Storytelling

Barbara M. Fisher

Madison • Teaneck
Fairleigh Dickinson University Press
London: Associated University Presses

© 1997 by Associated University Presses, Inc.

All rights reserved. Authorization to photocopy items for internal or personal use, or the internal or personal use of specific clients, is granted by the copyright owner, provided that a base fee of $10.00, plus eight cents per page, per copy is paid directly to the Copyright Clearance Center, 222 Rosewood Drive, Danvers, Massachusetts 01923. [0-8386-3740-X/97 $10.00 + 8¢ pp, pc.

Associated University Presses
440 Forsgate Drive
Cranbury, NJ 08512

Associated University Presses
16 Barter Street
London WC1A 2AH, England

Associated University Presses
P.O. Box 338, Port Credit
Mississauga, Ontario
Canada L5G 4L8

The paper used in this publication meets the requirements
of the American National Standard for Permanence of Paper
for Printed Library Materials Z39.48-1984.]

Library of Congress Cataloging-in-Publication Data

Fisher, Barbara (Barbara M.)
    Noble numbers, subtle words : the art of mathematics in the
science of storytelling / Barbara M. Fisher.
        p.   cm.
    Includes bibliographical references and index.
    ISBN 0-8386-3740-X (alk. paper)
    1. Numbers in literature. 2. Symbolism of numbers in literature.
3. Mathematics in literature. 4. Literature—History and criticism.
I. Title.
PN56.N86F57   1997
809'.93356—dc21   96-47598
                                                                          CIP

Library   PRINTED IN THE UNITED STATES OF AMERICA
University of Texas
at San Antonio

Contents

Acknowledgments

I should like to express my gratitude to several institutions for permission to reproduce the following materials:

"The Great Figure" by William Carlos Williams, from *Collected Poems: 1909–1939, Volume I*. Copyright © 1938 by New Directions Publishing Corporation.

I Saw the Figure 5 in Gold, by Charles Demuth, The Metropolitan Museum of Art, Alfred Stieglitz Collection.

Circle Limit IV by M. C. Escher, courtesy of Cordon Art, Baarn, Holland.

Woodcuts of "Philosophy" and "Mathematics" from Gregor Reisch, *Margarita Philosophica*, Freiburg, 1503, from the Rare Books and Manuscripts Division, The New York Public Library; Astor, Lenox, and Tilden Foundations.

A version of the chapter on *King Lear* appeared in *Journal of Dramatic Theory & Criticism* 4 (spring 1990).

The research for this book was supported in part by a grant from The City University of New York PSC-CUNY Research Award Program; and the passage from manuscript to book has been generously facilitated by Dean Martin Tamny, Division of Humanities, The City College of CUNY.

No book is written in a vacuum and this particular study could not have taken its shape without the help of colleagues and friends who debated its ideas, encouraged, challenged, and instructed me, and stimulated its development with their own thinking and ways of seeing things. I am grateful to my colleague in philosophy, Juliet Floyd, whose pioneer work on Wittgenstein and mathematics gave this study its fundamental frame of reference. Angus Fletcher contributed many initial insights, but one of his questions—What kind of word is a number?—opened an especially rich exploratory vein. I am beholden to distinguished Shakespeareans William Elton, Maurice Charney, and Joseph Wittreich for input on the *Lear* chapter, and to my colleague, the late Thomas King, for a careful reading of those pages. Two fine seventeenth-century scholars deserve my special thanks: John Shawcross helped greatly in focusing the Milton chapter and made many valuable suggestions; Samuel Mintz gave the revised chapter a close and sympathetic reading and helped to refine it. My colleague, Earl Rovit, read both the James and Borges chapters, and his thoughtful comments forced me to clarify certain passages. The chapter on Borges also derived enormous benefit from the careful readings and critiques of Gilberto Perez and Robert Ghiradella, and from the linguistic virtuosity of Magda Bogin. My esteemed colleagues, James de Jongh and James Hatch, generously took the time to read and comment helpfully on the Morrison chapter. Betty Rizzo, honored colleague and friend, read with scholarly care through the completed manuscript and I am indebted to her, as always, for kind encouragement and pointed questions. I imposed yet once more on the boundless generosity of Laury Magnus, who read the book as it developed, chapter by chapter, and it is impossible to know how much of her thinking is embedded in the final result. Not least, I have been singularly blessed in my editor, Wyatt Benner, whose expert counsel and meticulous work on the manuscript has been lit with an occasional gleam of humor.

I want to thank some bright young minds a little closer to home. Benji Fisher patiently explained various mathematical concepts, drew pictures, and explained again; without his lucidity in translating mathematical abstraction into image and language, this book could not have taken its present form. Ginda Kaplan Fisher, who knew all the time that Borges's *Aleph* pointed to Cantorian infinitudes, found ways to further clarify those concepts. Finally, I had the pleasure of associating with a brilliant young triumvirate (I thought of them as a private math/physics "brain trust") who courteously restrained their amusement, encouraged my project, and seemed always willing to monitor ideas and draw pictures: Jeremy Primer eased me into the mysteries of topology by way of bagels and various surfaces in my kitchen; David Rabson drew elegant miniature schematics to illustrate mathematical objects; and Joshua Burton, who introduced me to superstring theory the day before his wedding, foregrounded the notion of "tactful" numbers in the framework of diaspora and holocaust with all his extraordinary sensitivity to language. To all those named above, and to those others not named here who put their intelligence and knowledge at my service, I am deeply indebted.

Preface

The five studies that compose this book range in time over four hundred years and comprise genres as diverse as tragedy, epic poetry, the short story, the novel, and slave narrative, but they are all rooted in one simple idea. Each one springs from a way of looking at mathematics as an intrinsic component of language—that is, a specialized language within language—rather than as a discipline entirely separate and remote from the word. In this view, mathematics remains that part of language generally called upon for the precise expression of practical calculations and certain imaginative concepts. I am suggesting, then, that when mathematical elements are strongly present in a literary text, they contribute a necessary dimension to its language. Such elements may be used to formally shape the structure of a literary work, or they may inform a text in singular ways as agents and counteragents, as simple devices or transcendent abstractions. But above all, and in every case, they contribute to the linguistic force of the work.

In the chapters ahead, each of the primary texts draws into the narrative some aspect of number, geometry, or mathematical abstraction that deeply affects its meaning. To explore the functioning of such elements in a work of fiction, or poetry, or drama is to see that they contribute not only to the narrative frame, as in Borges's story, "The Aleph," but also to the development of character, as we will find in Toni Morrison's *Beloved*. An author may deploy mathematical elements to structure a metaphysics or—as in the case of Milton—to subtly enlarge on the problem of evil by casting its shadow, in effect, in figural terms. Most plainly put, I am proposing that mathematical objects can be used as shaping instruments for the purpose of vivid storytelling. To focus on this instrumentation in a given text is to illuminate its depth and complexity; at times, it will reorient the readings. However, it is not crystal clear to what extent such mathematical structuring is deliberate in the creation of a fiction and to what extent it may be intuitive. Is it conscious and strategic or purely irrational?

Even a cursory investigation shows that an author's use of mathematical elements falls into two general modes. On the one hand, there appears to be an unexceptional use of number, say, to designate quantity and measure; or a tactical use to heighten suspense, as in the "clocking" of a thriller; or to lend an actual or stylistic precision to a description. These choices made, or formulas invoked, seem to fall into the realm of conscious decision, although the decision may be as nearly automatic as the shifting of gears by an experienced driver. This mode is both informative and methodical: it supplies direct information of a quantitative nature and is received by the reader as such.

Not so the second mode, where number, numerical series, and geometric figuration serve a more surprising purpose: to contain and preserve powerful emotion. Here, whether the emotion is demonic hatred (as in *Paradise Lost*), frustrated erotic passion (as in "The Aleph"), seething anger (as in *Beloved*), a love-fear-death knot (as in *The Wings of the Dove*), or apocalyptic loss (as in *King Lear*), the mathematical element appears to contain the emotion, to hold it in place, so to speak, to preserve feeling in its purest intensity. In this case, the mathematical structuring functions somewhat like a lead crucible that confines a radioactive substance.

When Regan and Goneril taunt their father by decreasing his retinue of knights from one hundred to none, the paramount effect of their cold calculation is to capture an influx of hot rage. It may help to think about poets' use of a numerical structure to contain strong emotion if one recalls that two of the most passionate, deeply moving poems written in the twentieth century are cast in the intricate, mathematical villanelle form. Dylan Thomas's "Do Not Go Gentle into That Good Night," addressed to his dying, disapproving father, and Elizabeth Bishop's "One Art," concerning the ongoing loss of time, loved places, and beloved persons, both, confine the experience of anguish within a poetic form of utmost rigor. Several hundred years earlier, John Donne articulated the idea in a few terse lines:

> Griefe brought to numbers cannot be so fierce,
> For, he tames it, that fetters it in verse.
>
> But when I have done so,
> Some man, his art and voice to show
> Doth Set and sing my paine.

And, by delighting many, frees againe
Griefe, which verse did restraine.

It is my feeling, however, that in the medium of narrative the employment of this second, restraining, mode is largely intuitive on the part of the author and that it is received on an equally intuitive plane by the reader or listener.

The concluding study of this book shows Morrison's virtuoso deployment of both of the mathematical modes discussed here, while the chapter on Henry James's *Wings of the Dove* explores the various functions of geometry in that seductively difficult novel. It demonstrates James's use of geometric "blocks" (as he called them) to anchor the fragile web of relations, and his arrangements of squares and triangles to suggest connections between quartets and trios of characters in the most elegant—if invisible—way. I have shown, too, how James's spatial organization of the novel reveals the daemonic center of the piece and suggests, perhaps unexpectedly, who its true villain must be.

It should be apparent by now that this is not a study of "number symbolism," whether Pythagorean, Elizabethan, or cabalistic. There are fine extant studies of numerology in various literary contexts and I have referred to a number of them in the pages ahead, partly because one cannot focus on the presence of mathematics in literature without running into them, and sometimes because—as in the case of Borges—the intricacies of the Cabala exert a fascination upon the author. The creative work of the Oulipo group *(Ouvoir de littérature potentielle)*, who support mathematical and verbal experiment for its own sake, also falls outside the scope of this study. A work such as the *Invisible Cities* of Italo Calvino, one of its founding members, not only exemplifies but transcends the project of experiment. However, the intentional privileging of the mathematical element must exclude such texts from consideration here. The primary concern of this study is to explore the unpremeditated use of mathematics as a narrative tool—as a natural aspect of language—in the hands of a supremely gifted author. Most importantly, then, I want to preserve a theoretical distinction between contemporary experimentation with number in literature, or scholarly studies that reveal complex numerological significance, as for example in the works of Spenser, Milton, and Borges, and the present investigation into the use of "pure" mathematics in story and poem. If these studies demonstrate that the art of mathematics is a continuing presence in the venerable science of storytelling, this book will have served its purpose.

Rationalists, wearing square hats,
Think, in square rooms,
Looking at the floor,
Looking at the ceiling.
They confine themselves
To right-angled triangles.
If they tried rhomboids,
Cones, waving lines, ellipses—
As, for example, the ellipse of the half-
        moon—
Rationalists would wear sombreros.
                    —Wallace Stevens

The room in which I am lecturing is part of the physical world, and has itself a certain pattern . . . [but] "pure geometries" are independent of lecture rooms, or of any other detail of the physical world.
                    —G. H. Hardy, *A Mathematician's Apology*

   Subtle is the Lord . . .
                    —Einstein

NOBLE NUMBERS, SUBTLE WORDS

1

The Telltale
Figure

A classic joke about joking probes the cryptic, between-the-lines nature of humor by suggesting a kinship between storytelling and enumeration. A current version introduces it as "A Joke Whose Mathematical Flavor Does Not Arise Solely From The Numbers In It," and tells it this way:

> The young reporter, assigned to cover a jokewriter's convention, was expecting to hear some good stories. Instead, the featured comedian began to rattle off a series of numbers.
>
> "Ninety-three!" said the speaker, and the audience laughed. "Two hundred twelve!" They laughed again. "One thousand thirty-seven!" More laughter.
>
> The reporter couldn't stand it any longer. She nudged a nearby jokewriter and whispered, "What's going on?" "It's very simple," the jokewriter said. "Jokes are our business, and every joke in the world has been assigned a number. When the speaker says 'Ninety-three,' that means *joke* number ninety-three. So we laugh. Get it?" "You mean," asked the reporter dubiously, "you're going to crack up if I say to you, 'twenty-six'?" "No, no," said the jokewriter, "your delivery is wrong. Listen to this guy. He's good and you might learn something."
>
> So the reporter tried to appreciate the comedian's technique on 46, 989 and 2536. Then the comedian paused dramatically, waving his hands for silence. When he had the audience's full attention, he shouted "Ten thousand,—two hundred,—and three!" There was pandemonium. People were clapping and cheering. The jokewriter next to the reporter laughed so hard that tears ran down his face and he could hardly stand up.

19

"What happened? What happened?" the reporter demanded. "Why was that one so funny?"

"It's not just that it's funny," the jokewriter gasped. "The thing is, none of us ever heard that one before!"[1]

In the repertoire of funny stories, this particular joke depends upon the most general expectations of word and number—the qualitative information we expect from words, the ordering and encoding of information we connect with the simplest use of numbers. But as the leap of the "punch line" suggests, and because it is indeed, as the teller points out, a joke "Whose Mathematical Flavor Does Not Arise Solely From The Numbers In It," one senses a subtext that has little to do with general expectations, although it does reaffirm a common perception. That is, playing with numbers may well lead to a more specialized, more esoteric, more encrypted knowledge than is generally possessed— knowledge that requires training and a lexis outside the common reach. In fact, the reporter's confusion has nothing to do with numbers, as such; it merely demonstrates her ignorance of "insider" shoptalk. The reporter is on the outside. She just doesn't get it. From "underneath," it seems, this is a story about numbers from the mathematicians' point of view.

Or are we, as the raconteur suggests, seeing mathematics from the jokewriters' point of view? Clearly, there is more than one perspective. This study proposes a more open inquiry into the relations between numbers and storytelling than the joke permits. Very simply, we will be looking at some of the ways a gifted author turns mathematical concepts to literary use. The point is neither to elevate mathematics nor to mystify literature, but to expose a dimension of meaning in certain works of drama, epic poetry, and fiction that can only add to the pleasures of the text—or encourage new readings. Each of the five chapters ahead brings to the surface numerical, algebraic, or geometric concepts that already exist in a given text; in each, the mathematical construct radiates its special meanings into the work. For example, we will see how Shakespeare expands on two separate and antithetical notions of *zero*— "an O without a figure" as the Fool calls it—to structure a tragedy; how Milton draws on the most recent advances in seventeenth-century mathematics to effect the climactic transformation in the first book of *Paradise Lost*, and how the same poet deploys number, ratio, and figural letter-coding as intrinsic elements of the narrative. We will see the ways a novelist like Henry James uses Euclidean figures in designing what is perhaps his most intricate, most delicately contrived work of fiction;

and consider how a finely chiseled tale about romantic obsession may hinge upon a Cantorian mathematical abstraction, as in Borges's "The Aleph." Finally, we will investigate how Morrison's *Beloved*, a complex narrative having to do with slavery, genocide, and a destructive ghost, uses number and letter-coding to convey "unspeakable" information.

In effect, I am inviting the reader to consider number, algebraic letter-coding, geometric figuration, and mathematical abstractions as practical *literary* instruments. These mathematical concepts can be understood as specialized tools within the author's lexicon, just as mathematics itself is a specialized language within language. In this view, it doesn't make sense to think of mathematical ideas as absolutely unrelated to other supreme fictions, or to see number as antipathetic to the word. The joke about numbers-for-stories stresses the cryptic, enigmatic character of numerical manipulations, at least for the outsider. It may be helpful, at this point, to contrast the (fictional) treatment of numerals by the (fictional) jokewriters with the elegant treatment of a single number by a modern poet, and a modern painter.

William Carlos Williams's "The Great Figure" (1921) prompted Charles Demuth's brilliant painting, *I Saw the Figure Five in Gold* (1928). Together, the painting and the poem illustrate the multidimensional properties of number in an aesthetic context. With its visual echoes of the number five—a series of "fives" constant in design, yet diminishing in size as they recede inward, and enlarging outward almost past the picture plane—the painting seems to penetrate mathematical space. Demuth places the poet's name, "BILL," above the horizontal of the largest numeral, and the letter abbreviation for "number" (No.) within the curve of the five, graphically illuminating the relation of word to number. The cleanly executed graphics seem to honor abstract number itself, while the painting pays several kinds of tribute to its original stimulus—a poem charged with energy, color, and resonance, yet spare in form, precise in content, rich in signification. The thirteen lines of Williams's poem launch a powerful image:

> Among the rain
> and lights
> I saw the figure 5
> in gold
> on a red
> firetruck
> moving
> tense

unheeded
to gong clangs
siren howls
and wheels rumbling
through the dark city.[2]

"The Great Figure" closely conforms to Williams's famous definition of a poem as "a machine made of words." Each of its thirty-one

**Charles Demuth, *The Figure 5 in Gold*. Alfred Stieglitz Collection, The Met-
ropolitan Museum of Art.**

movable parts—that is, each individual word—functions as a precision-tooled component of the whole, while the "Great Figure" of the title introduces a wonderfully complex piece of verbal machinery. As a rhetorical "figure of speech," it announces the "howling" fire truck, the trope of the "unheeded" quintessential entity, and the poem, the figural "machine" itself. One of the more "clangorous" intonations of the Great Figure—its red and gold coloration—suggests the whore-of-Babylon splendor of the Church, so that on a subtle level, Williams's iconic fire-engine cartoons a religious emblem. The "figure 5" at the end of the third line contributes the abstract arithmetical sense of "figure," while the numeral itself stands apart as the poem's point of focus. Singled out typographically as a digit—not a number word—and underscored by terminal placement, the golden "5" is the object of the single sentence that constitutes the poem. It is the grammatical-mathematical object about which all the rest revolves. Reinforcing the centrality of the "5," Williams has chosen a numeral that occurs at the center or half-way point among the digits that compose the decimal system. On a metaphysical level, the moving but unmoved figure projects the notion of constancy in the midst of flux—not a new idea, even according to Aristotle: "[F]or in mathematics motion is a fiction, as the phrase goes, no mathematical entity being really moved *(kineisthai)*."[3] In the most graphic sense, then, the "5" exists as the unmoved/moving *object* and symbolic *subject* of this modernist poem. But it is the complex term "figure" that sounds a chord, as it were, simultaneously joining the verbal and visual arts to the mathematical like a C-major triad.

Count On It

We are in a position now to consider the familiar notions of "hard" number and "soft" word, and to remark on two or three words—such as *figure*—that in a number of languages contain both (hard) numerical and (soft) narrative senses. This phenomenon goes back, it may well be, to a time in the history of these languages when letter and number shared a common symbol system—an alphabet or syllabary. Discussing the evolution of Greek mathematics after Pythagoras, historian Morris Kline notes that in the three hundred years from Thales to Euclid "the mathematicians paid no attention to computation, and this art made no progress." Kline then observes: "For some unknown reason the classical Greeks changed their way of writing numbers to the Ionic or Alexandrian system, which uses letters of the alphabet. This alphabet system was the most common one in Alexandrian Greek mathematics," and he adds, "It was also used in ancient Syria and Israel."[4]

In Greek, Syrian, and Hebrew, then, the first letter of the alphabet became the written symbol for the number "one." The very term "alphabet," from "alpha, beta" or "aleph, beth" yielded the numerals "one, two." The letters, representing sound values, composed words. The numbers, representing quantities, permitted calculations. Moreover, the preexisting phonemic alphabet was "well ordered": that is, it possessed discrete symbols and a built-in continuity, both necessary for arithmetic purposes. In his encyclopedic work on the history of number symbols, Karl Menninger remarks: "The gradation of the number sequence is achieved by giving names to the elements of the sequence; these elements no longer remain anonymous and undifferentiated [as "strokes"] but form the steps of a staircase: Seven is 'higher' than three. In this staircase 'ten' plays the part of a threshold, or a landing."[5] While the alphabetic symbol system generated both the "soft" and the "hard" meanings for practical everyday uses, the congeniality of word and number also lent force to the development of mystical numerology, such as the rabbinical practice of *gematria* (the manipulation of number in the interpretation of Scripture), although mystical and sacred uses of number lore had existed since before the Chaldeans.[6] In the chapter called "Algebra and Fire," we will see that the notion of the numerical "staircase" and the cabalistic uses of number help to illuminate Jorge Luis Borges's tale, "The Aleph," with its visionary experience located on the threshold of "the nineteenth step."

The most elementary use of number in language is to express measure and quantity with precision. By convention, number signifies absolute values. It is the most concrete, most abstract, most constant, most inflexible, most rigidly invariable component of language. The concrete nature of number makes possible applications that range from household records to computerized information systems, and (beyond application) to the imaginative and aesthetic flights of pure theory. Significantly, it is the *identicality* of numerical units, the $1 + 1 + 1 = 3$ (that is, three identical "ones") that forms the foundation for absolute, unchanging values. We can count on it. Absolutely.

Words have a different character. They have a certain plasticity, the ability to project multiple meanings and to express subjective conditions. Written letter symbols permit the whole range of phonetic gradation and the whole intricate alternation of sound and silence in time (speech rhythms). Again, while the letter symbols do not require it, they permit the use of cadence to secure subtle variations in the meaning of voiced words or to musically indicate the difference, for example, between a question and a statement. Like snails bearing their shell-houses, words carry their etymological genesis and family history along with them. A glance at the *OED* shows that different connotations of a word may come to the forefront over time, while its denotation may undergo radical change; Andrew Marvell's "coy" mistress is coy in a very different way in the seventeenth century than she would be in the fifteenth or the twentieth. Again, a given word (as the English "cleave" or "bound") may contain directly antithetical senses, triggered by context.[7] The meaning of a spoken word may be altered ("colored") by tone or gesture or facial expression, while an ironic usage—whether spoken or written—can change the sense of a word or phrase into its direct opposite. Unlike numbers, words are eminently flexible, multidimensional, and capable of ironic twists and ambiguities; they have an uncanny ability to *sustain paradox*. Nevertheless, while they are capable of conveying subtle shades of meaning, they can also denote objective states, signal cultural attitudes, and express logical relations. Bakhtin has shown the extent to which dialogical warfare obtains between the various languages *(heteroglossia)* existing within a given linguistic matrix.[8] Syntax, which orders the words, provided grammarians *(mathematikoi)* in the classical period with the first systematic logic. On the other hand, poets may freely interfere with syntactic rules and disjunct syntax is fully acceptable in verse. But it is doubtless the *music* of spoken language, its essential rhythms, its innate metrics, that has inspired poets in all periods and places to compose "noble numbers." And rap.

For poets and storytellers the word is a supple and complex medium. Yet language in its infinite wisdom contains words that merge numerical with verbal meanings. In English, for instance, we use *account, accounting, tell* and *tale* in both narrative and quantitative senses. The "teller" tells a "tale," relates a story—or tells, tallies, i.e., counts up, the *tale of monies* behind the teller's window at the bank—just as a nun "tells" her rosary beads one by one. Shakespeare's "remembrance of things past" sonnet (sonnet 30) strikingly, tellingly, deploys the doubleness of "tell" and "account" when it reminds us that memory can "from woe to woe tell o'er / The sad account of forebemoanèd moan." Edgar Allen Poe's "The Tell-Tale Heart," a story about murder, dismemberment, and madness, suggests in both title and content that the meeting ground of both counting and telling lies in repeated rhythms: the heavy knocking at a door, the beating of a disembodied heart.

More recently, film critic Gilberto Perez has pointed out that the "hard" and "soft" aspects of these dyadic terms are not confined to English. Analyzing the dialectics of narrative continuity, he notes: "To recount means to tell as well as to count again; an account can be a computation or a narrative. The same word, *contar*, means in Spanish both to count and to tell; *compter* and *conter* are almost the same word in French, as are *zählen* and *erzählen* in German."[9] Telling is like counting, not in content but in form: "[A] story is told in succession, one thing and then another and then another, as things are counted. It may be," Perez conjectures, "that we tell about things that happened one after another, with the succession of the telling corresponding to the order of events in time, as we count a row of objects following their order in place."[10] In any case, it would seem that "counting" and "telling" once shared a single crib, so to speak. It is the term "figure," however, that functions as the richest conceptual nexus. "Figure" combines not only numerical and rhetorical senses, as one finds in the William Carlos Williams poem discussed earlier, but conveys explicitly visual imagery as well as a formidable array of other meanings. I want to examine this word, and *figura*, its ancestor, before remarking on the capacity of two cardinal numbers—zero and one—that have been deployed in English literary contexts as *figurae*.

The *Oxford English Dictionary* devotes three full pages to the word "figure," which derives from Latin *figura*, meaning "form" or "shape." Its stem is *fig-* (the *n*-less form of *fingere*), from the word for "potter." Hence, the primary senses of "figure" go back to the physical shaping, designing, and ornamenting of the potter's craft. The notion of a well-shaped physical object is apparent in the English phrase, "a fine figure," meaning a well-shaped body or "cutting a fine figure" which idiomatically reproduces the original sense of making a fine "impression." Perhaps the physical sense is conveyed most forcefully by the negative term, *dis*figurement, or mutilation. The *OED* also connects both English "figure" and Latin *figura* with Greek *schema*, which similarly denoted "form" and "shape," but includes an intellective aspect as well. One sees these parent senses still in force in English "figure" when its sense of "design" means to *scheme* or to *calculate* in a scheming manner. Erich Auerbach, whose monograph on the term remains a philological gem, tells us that "side by side with the original signification [of *figura*] and overshadowing it, there appeared a far more general concept of grammatical, rhetorical, logical, mathematical—and later even of musical and choreographic—form."[11]

Like *figura*, its etymological ancestor, English "figure" acts something like a verbal lens that gathers and concentrates diverse yet oddly related rays of meaning—all within the limits of a six-letter word. In this context, Wittgenstein's concept of "family resemblance" in his philosophy of language is perhaps the most useful model for grasping such a phenomenon—for "figure" summons up an entire clan of meanings.[12] The family of meanings ranges from the physical to the pictorial to the rhetorical to the purely mathematical, as Auerbach points out, depending upon its linguistic context. Webster lists seventeen such contexts for the noun form alone; alphabetically ordered, they include arithmetic, astrology, dance, finance, geometry, graphic arts, logic, music, and rhetoric. The mathematical sense of "figure" remains characteristically concrete, like the integer or numeral it denotes. The substantive (as "the figure five") gives an unchanging, stable, utterly fixed quantitative symbol, while the verbal "to figure" means to calculate, either using those same symbols or mentally. In addition, the colloquial uses of "figure" include (1) to "figure on" (count on); (2) "to figure out" (analyze); and (3) "to figure up" (add up a total). Each of these locutions indicates a mental activity related to arithmetic operations—or to scheming. Clearly, they share a marked family resemblance. Just as clearly, with Auerbach's help, we see that the concept of "figure" is exceptional in the capacity to generate a cluster of definitions, to capture, codify, and disseminate very specific information from separate and distinct sites of meaning. Which brings us to a pair of *figurae*, the particular graphic symbols that Milton has chosen, in book 1 of *Paradise Lost*, to convey a cluster of distinct meanings.

As graphic symbols, both letter and number have a pictorial or "figural" dimension. In the system of European languages, for example, X and T suggest crossing, Y a meeting of paths, S the image of a serpent. The familiar Roman numerals supply another graphic example of figural crossover. The single-stroke letter I symbolizes "one," V is "five" and X means "ten." The letter C (for *centum*) is the number "one hundred," so that the "Comedian" in the title of Wallace Stevens's poem, *The Comedian as the Letter C*, takes on a connotation of wholeness, of a harmonious full count, as well as other hermeneutic possibilities.[13]

In English however, and in English alone, two letter symbols—O and I—not only correspond to the numerical symbols for "zero" and "one" but also function as individual words. Zero doubles as the vocative "O" and the exclamatory "O!" (both of which point to extraordinary objects), while the notation for the number "one" easily doubles as the first-person singular, the "I" of identity. The two primary symbols of the digital system, therefore, project multiple resonances in English. Add to these the Freudian geometry of gender in the round circle and vertically erect line; or the Pythagorean notion that "ten" is the number of perfection—that is, the pairing of 1 and 0 constitutes a mystical completion—and we find the round zero and the linear one have become *figurae*. They encode complex information that extends from pure geometric abstraction to quantitative and visual values to cryptic sexual imagery. How seductive such a pair might be for an English poet!

Milton deploys the circular zero and linear one at several strategic moments in the first book of his epic, as we shall see. While such moments are rhetorically rich—each woven into an epic simile—his choice of symbols promotes the idea of a theodicy structured with mathematical precision. Together, the zero and the one become figural archetypes associated with Satan and his fallen legions. It is worth noting, in context, that Shakespeare has also used the figure "O" at times in a primarily graphic sense, and not solely in *King Lear*. Cleopatra's dream of the absent love object, in act 5 of *Antony and Cleopatra*, is a case in point:

> His face was as the heavens, and therein stuck
> A sun and moon, which kept their course, and lighted
> The little O, the earth.
>
> (5.2.79–81)

The "O" projects a graphic image of a spherical planet. However, if one hears it voiced dramatically as an Elizabethan "O-groan,"[14] it also conveys Cleopatra's anguish, while as a zero figure it symbolizes nothingness and absence—the "nothing" she is left with, the absence of the lover. In English poetry and drama, then, the letter-numbers O/zero and I/one may well exist as telltale figures: designed, choreographed, accountable.[15]

In exploring the use of number and algebraic letter-coding in a literary context, one should note that a storyteller—whether Elizabethan or contemporary—may use numerical constructs in very different ways, and for two distinct purposes, as we will see in Morrison's remarkable treatment of number in *Beloved*. The question that must arise is whether an author's deployment of number in a fiction is conscious and deliberate or whether it derives purely from aesthetic intuition—and to what extent, if any, these modes coincide. As noted earlier, number can be employed for simple enumeration, or perhaps to suggest a lack of feeling, or to lend a stylistic or actual precision to a description, or to heighten suspense, as in the "clocking" of the action in a detective story. These are deliberate, "strategic" uses of number in composing a fiction. On the other hand, one may find number used to structure episodes of great dramatic intensity, as we find in the germinal passage from *King Lear* (act 2, scene 4) taken up in the following chapter. In such a case, one cannot be certain as to whether the use of numerals and number words is intentional, partly intentional, or purely intuitive. My feeling is that it is a purely intuitive aesthetic decision, although number seems to be used at such moments in a formal, measured way. It serves to contain and enclose powerful emotion, while the dialogic interplay of number word and word tends to suggest limits but also to preserve the intensity of feeling. As against the trivializing, sentimentalizing, near-comic scenes of melodrama, what is achieved at such moments is genuine inexorable drama. This brings us to the question of "inexorability," to Wittgenstein's observations on the uses of mathematics in language, and to the idea of literary language games as forms of life.

INVENTED "FORMS OF LIFE"

In approaching Wittgenstein's notion of "language games" as "forms of life," and his conviction that use is the authentic determinant of meaning, I want to take under consideration what mathematics and ordinary language may have in common. The term "mathematics" and the designation of "mathematician" derive from the Greek *mathein*, a form of *mantháno*, which denotes a very specific kind of knowing—to learn by inquiry. It describes the desire to "find out about a thing," to reach out for knowledge. Almost from the very beginning, *mathésis* referred to an act of questioning, on the one hand, and to an attitude of active reception, on the other. It meant to ascertain, then to perceive and comprehend. As the pursuit of an intellective desire, *mathésis* results in certain test objects, so to speak. It might be a mathematical puzzler such as Fermat's Last Theorem, recently solved, it appears, after 350 years of ardent mathematical inquiry.[16] Or, cast into language, *mathésis* may blossom into the kind of philosophical inquiry known as "Socratic dialogue"—an open-ended attempt to define as precisely as possible what people mean when they use such terms as "love" or "piety" or "justice"—still an object of study after two-and-a-half millennia.

From the outset the pursuit of mathematical knowledge could win entry into an elite inner circle. Kirk and Raven, in *The Presocratic Philosophers*, point out that after the death of Pythagoras, his school "divided into two sects, one of which, the so-called 'Acousmatists' [Listeners] preserved the mystical side of his teaching, while the other, the

'Mathematicians,' concentrated on the scientific side."[17] The Mathematicians, it seems, were the insiders who shared the central mysteries of the cult, while the Listeners constituted the devotees who remained outside the initiates' circle—not unlike the relation of our jokewriters to the uninitiated reporter. At the same time we know from Herodotus, who distinguishes a "mathematical line" from a "physical line," that by the classical period geometry could be perceived as an abstract, ideational, fully independent science.

In any case, the evolution of logical-mathematical relations from the relational principles of grammar—the ordering "rules of syntax"—and the existence of ratios, equivalencies, identical repetition, number and measurement words in ordinary speech have all continued to link the mathematical discipline to its matrix in language. In fact, as late as the Hellenistic period a *mathematikos* might be understood as a "grammarian" or, in philosophical terms, as a rigid "dogmatist." The title of the Hellenistic treatise, *Adversus mathematicos (Kata mathematikoi)*, by Sextus Empiricus (which sets forth skeptical arguments against dogmatic claims to absolute truth) may be translated as "Against the Dogmatists" or "Against the Grammarians" with greater validity than "Against the Mathematicians."[18] Finally, E. A. Sophocles' *Greek Lexicon of the Roman and Byzantine Periods* indicates that *ta mathémata* denoted mathematics *and* astrology, and a *mathematikos* of that period was a mathematician or an astrologer, probably both. This is hardly surprising when one considers the unbroken connection of mathematics with astronomy *and* with the science of prediction, and when one takes into account the precise calculation and the facility in geometry that astrology requires.

Although mathematics grew into a full-fledged discipline a long time ago, its early connections with the larger matrix of language are still apparent in the fields of logic, mathematical metaphysics, quantitative linguistics, Chomskian transformational grammar, and information theory—as well as in the art of poetry, the murder mystery, and various other contexts of drama and fiction. Mathematical physics joined itself to literature to the extent of adopting the Joycean "quark" to designate a subatomic particle. For the most part, however, the denizens of language and mathematics have preferred to occupy their separate domains. There are exceptions, of course, rare individuals who seem to take pleasure in using both sides of the bicameral organ, such as the fourth-century philosopher, Hypatia, who made significant contributions to the study of Euclidean conic sections, on the one hand, and discoursed on fine points in Plato and Aristotle, on the other. Indeed, the list is notably extranational.

In the pages ahead we will find the Argentinian writer Borges expounding the genius of the Persian Omar Khayyam, both in algebra and rhymed quatrains. There is the remarkable Benjamin Banneker, the eighteenth-century African American farmer who became a mathematician and astronomer, and who couched arithmetic problems in the form of verse.[19] There are the immortal *Alice* books, bizarre landscapes of logic turned to Carrollian fiction. There is Henri Bergson, mathematician and philosopher, who produced a classic work on the theory of comedy; and the disturbing, groundbreaking, mathematically sophisticated Charles Sanders Peirce, who fathered the philosophy of pragmatism, developed systematic notions of Firstness, Secondness, and Thirdness—and critiqued the theological writings of Henry James Sr. with sardonic acerbity and a certain appreciation. There is the slim but inspired volume, *Poetry and Mathematics*, by the American Scott Buchanan.[20] There is Roman Jakobson, whose Cartesian axes transformed linguistic studies of metaphor and metonymy, and who devoted some thought to "Signe Zéro"; there is I. A. Richards's *Science and Poetry*, and the New Critics' adaptation of quasi-mathematical formulations in the analysis of texts. And there is Viennese-born Ludwig Wittgenstein, philosopher and logician, a mathematician respected by Frege and Russell; an engineer trained in aeronautics; a German soldier in the First World War, and a prisoner of war; a teacher of elementary school children in rural Austria, and the compiler of a dictionary for their use; a designer of the Bauhaus School; an amateur sculptor with an exquisite ear for music; a hermit and ascetic and philanthropist; a gardener at a monastery; a catcher and trainer of birds; a medical orderly and laboratory assistant; an inquisitor of Shakespeare; a lover of Schubert and German romantic poetry; and a devotee of American Westerns. He electrified the positivists of the Vienna Circle and debated with Alan Turing, who conceived the first computer or "information machine"; G. E. Moore, the dean of moral philosophy at Cambridge, attended his lectures. Something of a pragmatist and something of a mystic, Wittgenstein was reclusive, a relentless perfectionist, a restless revisionist, an iconoclast, an originator. "What does it mean to *believe* Goldbach's theorem?" he asks—not a mathematician's question. "A mathematician is bound to be horrified by my mathematical comments," he observes in *Philosophical Grammar*, "since he has always been trained to avoid indulging in thoughts and doubts of the kind I develop."[21] Often disturbed and almost always disturbing, he taught philosophy at Cambridge and changed the whole course of academic thinking about "ordinary" language.[22]

Wittgenstein's thinking moved from the "logical space" and "atomic facts" of the *Tractatus* to an almost sociological examination of the dynamics of speech in various collaborative contexts.[23] People engaged in "language games"—that is, they learned and then delivered habitual responses at given language sites—on the job, at school, making friends, and so forth. Wittgenstein invented study models for the purpose: strange "tribes" whose language was severely limited, workers who moved at the pointing of a finger, people who set a dinner table with the right number of plates, forks, and spoons, without taking the trouble to count out each set of objects. He questioned the "inexorability" of mathematical constructs and projected an engineer's understanding of the material world by suggesting that there might be a use for an adaptable measuring rod, a flexible footrule.[24] He asked strange, penetrating questions about rules and games: "If there is no queen, can the game still be called chess?" He opposed "the subliming of our whole account of logic," and the Platonic notion of number as an a priori and transcendent existant.[25] He seriously suggested that a philosophy could be constructed entirely of jokes. Language was a living organism for Wittgenstein—"to imagine a language means to imagine a form of life"—but it was also an adversary with siren entrapments and an occult power of its own: "Philosophy is a battle against the bewitchment [*Verhexung*] of our intelligence by means of language."[26] Above all, and linked in his own mind to the enchantments of language, Wittgenstein has the mathematician's perception of mathematics as an *aesthetic* pursuit. A note to himself, written in 1936, remarks the "queer resemblance between a philosophical investigation (perhaps especially in mathematics) and an aesthetic one."[27]

Juliet Floyd glosses these aspects of Wittgenstein's thinking as they are formulated in his *Remarks on the Foundations of Mathematics*. In Wittgenstein's view, as she points out, "what *compels* us to count the way we do is our participation in the practice, the culture, of counting."[28] In the *Remarks*, Wittgenstein opposes practical "usability" to mathematical "truth" in his observations concerning a numerical series: "It can't be said of the series of natural numbers—any more than of our language—that it is true, but: that it is usable, and, above all, *it is used*."[29] In the context of the present study—an investigation of the uses of mathematics in various "language games" of literature—Floyd's commentary is instructive:

> The parallel with "our language" is the first explicit indication
> in *RFM* of the Wittgensteinian notion . . . that "number" is a gram-

matical category; i.e., that our counting takes place, not in a vacuum, but within the context of a living language. . . . Rather than claiming that the series of natural numbers exists, or that we have knowledge of it, or that it is an infinite series [and then attempting to justify his claim], Wittgenstein observes that the series is, above all, *used*.[30]

In the "form of life" that exists as a poem or play or shaped narrative, whether it concerns a mythic hero such as the Celtic Cuchulainn; or a romantic love-suicide like Goethe's young Werther; or an old king who does not really understand power until he becomes its wretched victim; or a fabulously wealthy young girl who learns that her days are numbered; or yet again, an escaped slave who must decide on the spot whether her baby daughter is better off dead or alive—in the invention of such forms of life, mathematical constructs and geometric figures function as necessary elements of living language.[31] To consider the deployment of number, the emblem-value of geometric forms, and the coherence afforded by abstract mathematical concepts represents a challenge. Not every literary artifact is so structured, but for those that contain a mathematical dimension, to be aware of it means to expose contrapuntal designs and harmonic resonances that can profoundly reorient the readings. In *Remarks on the Foundations of Mathematics*, Wittgenstein suggests an intimate relation between mathematics and fiction: "The mathematician is an inventor, not a discoverer."[32] At another point he observes, "A poet cannot really say of himself 'I sing as the birds sing'—but perhaps Shakespeare could have said this of himself."[33] And he asks: "Was he perhaps a *creator of language* rather than a poet?"

2

Zero Reason,
Infinite Need

The voice of the devil, in Blake's *Marriage of Heaven and Hell* (1790–93), expounds the right relation of reason to energy: "Energy is the only life and is from the Body; and Reason is the bound and outward circumference of Energy."[1] The proposition figures here as a deliberate heresy, an ironic reversal that moves Reason from the center of things to the outer limits. Yet it suggests a principle of order, a geometric containment of violent energies—form as the limit of force. In the historic sense, the voice issues out of the whirlwind of the French Revolution, and Blake's proposition is uttered in the spirit of prophecy. Within its boundaries, the great contraries of passion and restraint are brought together and "married."

Essentially the same proposition, its second axiom in particular— "Reason is the bound and outward circumference of Energy"—is dramatized with uncanny precision in *King Lear*, conceived some 180 years earlier. While the mood of Shakespeare's play is apocalyptic, it too is concerned with prediction and prophecy, it too develops an ironic cosmic vision, though it entails a darker, bitterer, more sardonic joke than the romantic's reversal of angelic and demonic orders. More importantly for the purpose of this study, one scene in *King Lear* stands apart as perhaps *the* most elegant model in literature of a dramatic episode structured by a mathematical calculus. Put most simply, the scene we are about to examine is constructed in such a way that number—concrete impersonal number—functions as the "bound and outward circumference" of an intense surge of emotional energy.

In act 2, scene 4, Regan and Goneril "disquantity" Lear of his retinue. The audience does not actually see the dismissal of the knights but is present at the verbal rape of Lear's manpower. Certainly the two raptor children seem as unnatural as Lot's daughters, but they twist in the opposite direction. Instead of lying with their father they seek to unman him. We therefore watch these daughters taunt and tease, openly calculate, swiftly reduce the last vestige of the king's authority to nought.[2]

The entire calculus of *Lear*—that is, its choice of sign and symbol, its emotional economy, its computation of identity, its balance of proportion and disproportion, in a word, its *reckoning*—can be derived from this focal passage. For Regan and Goneril's heartless game leads directly to Lear's celebrated "O! reason not the need" speech, and a close look reveals that the passage that ends scene 4 is unusual in several respects. Not only does it touch on every major theme in the tragedy, so that the reason/need speech serves as an index to the play's main concerns, but it establishes the strongest vantage points from which to observe the action. The impatient old man and his scheming offspring physically embody the two extremes of perspective that determine the course of events. Most pointedly, the passage demonstrates the dramatic deployment of number words and a numerical progression to suggest rational structures, on the one hand, and a moment-to-moment shifting of the boundaries of reason, on the other. Indeed, the most striking *formal* element in the passage is its controlled counterpoint of energetic word and rational number.

The section I have in mind runs from line 247 to line 284 (Arden edition, 1972), from Lear's "I gave you all—!" to his final overwrought utterance before the storm: "but this heart / Shall break into a hundred thousand flaws / Or ere I'll weep. O Fool! I shall go mad."[3] At the center of the passage is Lear's uttered "O!"—a single symbol that encodes three separate kinds of information. Quite literally, the "O" stands in the place of three separate signs, linked like three separate Graces into one round iconic form. The scene is organized in such a way as to draw a numerical fencework around an intolerable upsurge of feeling. Whether intuitively or deliberately, the dramaturge is using number, the prime instrument of reason and measure, to circumscribe a dangerous explosion of energy. Number so used, in conjunction with a certain kind of geometric structuring, functions in a dramatic context like a retaining wall. Measure for measure, it preserves the affective content in its pure undilute intensity. As a chalice may hold strong wine or strong poison, so may the framing surround of number act to contain strong emotion and conserve its initial potency. We are in a position now to look more closely at the arithmetic guideposts that lead into the "disquantity" passage in act 2, and then to open the lens, as it were, to survey the structuring geometry of *King Lear*.

The orchestration of word and number in act 2 begins almost imperceptibly at line 131 with a proportion, a ratio of infelicity, that in itself predicts an equivalence between the sisters. We are shown an identity that will all too soon be confirmed as fact—and this is achieved by means of a *syntactic* mirror image. Having left Goneril's house vowing never to return, Lear encounters Regan, from whom he expects gratitude and hospitality. He exclaims, "Thy sister's naught: O Regan! . . ." "Naught" means nothingness, lacking in worth, zero spelled out, while the "O" to the right of the colon, supported by the exclamation point, clearly indicates an ejaculation.[4] And while the word *zero* occurs nowhere in Shakespeare, we can see that here, as elsewhere, the letter "O" provides not only a graphic but a phonic representation of the cipher. In other words, whether it is read silently in the text or voiced on stage, the "O" roundly suggests nothingness, emptiness, just like the word "naught." In this case, the very syntax becomes a semiotic device. It tells us that the playwright is insinuating Sophoclean irony in the subtlest, most elegant form—the form of a mathematical proportion. The audience, or the reader, is allowed to glimpse in advance what the protagonist is on the verge of discovering: "As G has proven worthless, so nothing worth will prove R." In fact, the "ratio" predicts in the most economical way that the immediate future will mirror the immediate past; soon enough, we will find the emptied father standing like an invisible "mean" between these two extremely rational dames.

One must ask at this point if so much meaning may rightly be extracted from syntax, or ascribed to single letters or to highly variable elements of punctuation—as a colon must be in an Elizabethan text. Aren't these elements merely the particles of scripted language? Before moving to the passage in scene 4 that is our primary concern, it will be helpful to briefly consider the notion of microstructure.

In *King Lear and the Gods*, his classic study of pagan and theological elements in the play, William Elton underscores the importance of its structural devices. These constitute "a tacit commentary which the dramatist, operating *ab extra*, may legitimately introduce," so that, according to Elton, "juxtapositions . . . themselves may take on meaning."[5] Elton is referring to the grand structures of *Lear*, the sequencing of dialogue and event, the *liaison des scènes*. But as Angus Fletcher has persuasively shown in the case of *Othello*, the playwright's shaping may be all-pervasive, touching anything and everything that might yield meaning, reinforce meaning, or complicate the meaning. Certainly, when the dramatist is a consummate poet—and one whom Dr. Johnson singled out as unable to resist the pun, or "quibble"—one may expect elements of sequence and juxtaposition to be as meaningful, at times, at the level of syllable play and letter shape as it is on the larger, more visible surface. And in fact, there can be no question as to Shakespeare's intentional deployment of single letters in *King Lear*. We are alerted to his methodical letter play early in act 2 when Kent furiously challenges Oswald: "Thou whoreson zed! Thou unnecessary letter!" (2.2.61). A more significant signal is the initial letter-number equivalence established in act 1 when Lear's Fool confronts his master: "now thou art an O without a figure. I am better than thou art now; I am a Fool, thou art nothing" (1.4.189-91).

It is precisely at this linguistic sublevel, at the level of particles, that Fletcher finds both the redeeming music and the fatal metaphysic of *Othello*. In one study of that play, he shows how Shakespeare "chooses one vowel, the O-sound, for continual linguistic transformation. He takes this initially meaningless phoneme, O, and gradually changes it into a more and more obviously meaningful morphemic unit, an O that 'means something.'"[6] Arguing that Shakespeare "moves his play, and us, slowly toward a new perception, that Death itself is the only hero of tragedy," Fletcher concludes: "The phonemically meaningless O is transformed, by weaving iteration, into a perdurable sense. O is at last only a signature of unadulterated woe, pain beyond pain, dreadful loss."[7]

Attention to this performative aspect of the "O" (almost in J. L. Austin's linguistic sense of the term) and the recognition of its power as staged utterance begins, one should note, with Maurice Charney's restoration of critical significance to the "O-groans" in *Hamlet*. In a seminal paper, Charney reinvoked the dimension of the spoken utterance in actual performance. He sharply reminded textual scholars that the O-vowel functioned not only as a graphic sign, meaningful within a quarto or folio text, but as a sound-in-itself meaningful to actors and audience: "Opinions about the O-groans seem to depend on what moves us in the theater, how we define poetry, and the way we conceive Hamlet as a dramatic character."[8] Charney underscored the singular "unquotability" that parallels the emotional density of the O-sound in Elizabethan tragedy: "The O-groans are painful, not mellifluous, and this applies equally to Hamlet, King Lear, Lady Macbeth. . . . When rendered effectively on stage, they are disturbing without being quotable. . . ."[9] It is at this critical level of linguistic particles, of heard sound and isolated elements, that we are now able to approach the passage in which Lear, as profoundly as Othello, experiences his pain beyond pain, his dreadful loss.

As the action develops in act 2, scene 4, Regan advises her father to apologize to Goneril and return to her for the duration of his month's stay. Lear's reply advances the mathematical "argument" of the scene. "Never, Regan. / She hath abated me of half my train" says Lear, calling upon number to defend his reason (2.4.155–56). In fact, Lear has evidently disregarded Goneril's injunction to lessen his force by half, for following the entrance of Oswald with Goneril, he tells her, "I can be patient; I can stay with Regan, / I and my hundred knights" (2.4.228–29). But Regan, counter to Lear's expectations, now proposes to her father to "mingle reason with your passion," and with that initiates the scene's fateful countdown. "What! fifty followers? / Is that not well? What should you need of more?" In Regan's line, we see that *need* has been posited as directly contrary to *reason*, just as "passion" is reason's contrary in the earlier speech. But the game is just begun, and the term *need* will reappear in the mouth of each one of the three participants before the grim farce ends. Almost immediately, Regan chops "so great a number" in half. Should Lear come to her, he is to "bring but five-and-twenty; to no more / Will I give place or notice" (2.4.246–47). And Lear says, "I gave you all. . . ." I shall do no more than draw attention here to the quiet accumulation of absolutes as the dialogue gains speed—*naught, never, all*—absolutes that resonate, re-sound those framing the tragedy: the five "nothings" of act 1, the five "nevers" of act 5.[10]

The collaboration between word and number word grows more marked as the scene progresses. Lear decides to abjure Regan and her five-and-twenty and turns back to the daughter he has cursed. "I'll go with thee," he tells Goneril, "Thy fifty yet doth double five-and-twenty, / And thou art twice her love" (2.4.257–58). Notice the dimension of double meaning built into Lear's "double" at line 257, its sense of duplicity and collusion on the one hand, and, on the other, its hint of the sisters' identicality, their innate sameness. In truth, nought doubled yields twice as much nothingness as before and the selfsame quantity, all at once. The sisters, now unbraked by decorum and harnessed to a chilling logic, respond by speeding up the process of subtraction:

> GON.   Hear me, my Lord,
> What need you five-and-twenty, ten, or five,
> To follow in a house where twice so many
> Have a command to tend you?

REG.   What need one?
LEAR.   O! reason not the need. . . .

                                                    (258–62)

Lear's "O!" at the opening of line 262 is the beginning of the an-
guished speech that brings the scene virtually to its close. But in an
examination of the interplay of word and number word in *Lear*, one
must pause here and mark that the symbol "O" at this point is uniquely
central. Following hard on Regan's "What need *one*?" at the terminus
of the preceding line of dialogue, Lear's *"O!"* becomes as complex a
semiotic device as may be construed in a single symbol. How is the
reader to read it? How is the actor to voice it? What value should be
ascribed to each of the three radials of meaning it suggests? Consider
the possibilities:

1.   As part of the numerical structure of the scene, "O" unavoid-
ably carries the abstract mathematical sense of "naught": *zero*.
2.   As it marks the peak of an intense emotional crisis, the vowel
represents a howl, an Elizabethan "O-groan."
3.   As part of the larger structure of the drama, Lear's "O!" signals
the exact moment of anagnorisis in the tragedy, and the pivot of its
tragic reversal, the peripeteia. That is, Lear's "O!" occurs at the moment he perceives the truth, and what follows is the "turning point" or
irrevocable change that he must undergo as a result of that knowledge.
Hazlitt found the third act of *Othello* and the first three acts of *King Lear*
to be "Shakespeare's great master-pieces in the logic of passion." Surely
Lear's initial "O!" at line 262 records the moment of horrid revelation,
of damning insight—that critical point at which the protagonist cannot
but grasp the truth of his situation, the totality of his loss. It means "O!
I see!" And from that point on, for Lear, all is changed.

More information is thus compressed, like a microchip, within the
symbol "O" at this juncture than a single letter may be expected to hold.
In *Lear*, however, such triple-threat coding is not only probable but necessary, for the separate waves of meaning that ripple out from the "O"
connect the microstructures of this scene to the larger geometric framework of the tragedy. In *King Lear*, "nothing" is the generative concept
and the circle of "nothing" is weighted with dramatic meaning. In its
mathematical character, *naught* is the most abstract of the play's circular images. But, as we shall see, in its capacity as a positional notation,
or "holding place," the zero contains a built-in contradiction. As for the

word "nothing," it too propagates a healthy paradox in this play. In short, the circle of nothing does more than symbolize the mere absence of quantity, i.e., signify absolute zero. "Nothing" in *Lear*—from Cordelia's first utterance of the term—holds within itself the qualitative absolute "all."

Of course, the "disquantity" passage does not end with Lear's "O!" The velocity with which Regan and Goneril reduce his "century" of men (and, we suspect, his full span of years) continues to increase after the zero point is reached. Frustrated, stripped of illusion, harried beyond the threshold of restraint, Lear breaks into the impassioned speech that ends, as the external storm approaches, with a tremendous acceleration into the irrational, an infinite breaking and cracking—a fractionating regress into negative number and the void. His final words are a premonition of madness:

> I have full cause of weeping [Storm heard at a distance.]
>   but this heart
> Shall break into a hundred thousand flaws
> Or ere I'll weep. O Fool! I shall go mad.
>
>   (2.4.282–84)

The king's fortunes are inventoried at line 290 in Regan's final unconditional ruling. She will receive her father, "But not one follower." Not one.

The letter-coding in the lines shown immediately above repays careful attention. Double vowels and doubled consonants predominate. The two *ll*'s of "full," "I'll," "Shall," and "shall" indicate a liquid sound, the soft moan originating in the throat. For the reader, they graphically picture two identical figures standing side by side. Indeed, from Lear's initial "O! reason not the need" to the final syllables of his speech, the letter play reinforces our sense of double-dealing, blindness, and loss. As in *Othello*, the O-vowel proliferates. One is particularly struck by the double-o's of "poorest," "poor," "fool," and "O Fool!" peering like Gloucester's blinded eyes from the text. And it is hard to escape the echoic doublings in "weep," "weep," "weeping," "weep," or the same vowel-doubling in the ongoing reiteration of the word *need*. The sisters' tacit complicity has reduced their father to the status of a dependent. Both figuratively and literally they have "unmanned" him; and by virtue of the "woman's" tears he would not shed, Lear, in his own mind, is unsexed. Above all, the multiple letter doublings serve to cryptically underscore his daughters' duplicity and their identical aims.

This same passage, as noted earlier, touches on every critical issue in the play. Lear's "O! reason not the need" speech introduces themes of home and homelessness, broken filial decorums, calculating rhetoric and calculated aggression. It confronts human weakness, denial, blindness; it examines aging and insanity; arrogance and humility; vengefulness, bestiality, and insatiable greed. It touches on truth and the appearance of truth; being stripped and being clothed. Lear's speech concerns the king-as-fool, nature and the unnatural, kind and unkindness, and the terrifying topos of the world upside-down.[11] It rings forth notions of value: currency and exchange, emotional "coinage." At the last, Lear's calling upon his Fool, in conjunction with a breaking *heart*, poignantly suggests the presence-in-absence of Cordelia, the beloved and loving child, whose very name intimates heart (*cor, cordis*) and bond (cord), and the medicinal, healing effect of a cordial. Each of these themes fits into place somewhere between the quiet pole of reason and the unquiet pole of need.

The scene we have been examining so minutely stands forth as the most sharply etched example of a dramatic schema in which an otherwise uncontainable intensity of emotion is enclosed, hedged about, actually supported by number—and surrounded, as we shall see, by a more remote constellation of cosmic absolutes. But this particular scene also develops an independent drama of inverse ratio. As Fortune's wheel describes a half-turn in *Lear*, as poor forked unaccommodated man may be stripped and stood upside down, so in this scene are things pulled inside out. As his external forces are decreased, Lear's fury increases. The surge of negative emotion—rage and the desire for retribution—grows in inverse proportion to the lessening of external power. And as the opposed plate movements of a geological fault must eventually result in massive tectonic upheaval, so Lear must crack. The division of the kingdom has become the division of the king, separated from his men, from his daughters, from his reason.

From the standpoint of the protagonist, however, the dialectic of the passage entails a rapid, disorienting retrogression as energy converts from external power to internal rage. The numerical structure of the scene *and* Lear's catapult into negation can be expressed arithmetically as a progression from positive to negative number:

$$+100 \ldots O \ldots -100,000$$

That is, what began with Regan's proposal to reduce the king's bodyguard by half moves from the positive integer 100, Lear's original "century" of knights, through the zero/O at the opening of his speech, to the "hundred thousand flaws" at its close. This last is a number that indicates transfinite negation: Lear's heart is breaking into tenfold *myriads*, i.e., countlessness beyond mere uncountability. In the Hindu-Arabic notation (above), it can be seen as the digit one, preceded by the minus sign, and followed by five zeros, a series of *five nothings*. In sum, it would appear that the center of the numerical progression, the emotional peak of scene four, and the turning point or peripeteia of the play—all three—can be located in the "O" at line 262.

ZERO, CIRCLE, SPHERE

The geometry of *Lear* is round. Its plot, germinated by dark amorality, continues to swell and grow "round-womb'd" as Edmund's unwed mother. Its worldview anticipates Vico, involving great cycles of history. Its dramatic continuum is as curved as Einsteinian space-time; at its end an old man has grown boy: "Pray you, undo this button" (5.3.308).[12] Its action, focused at the beginning on what may well have been a round map, spirals like a vortex toward an elegiac finale.[13] Coleridge, in fact, compared the action of *King Lear* to "the hurricane and the whirlpool, absorbing while it advances," while Hazlitt likened the king's embattled mind to "a sharp rock circled by the eddying whirlpool that beats and foams against it." Included in the play's circular imagery is the identifying ring Cordelia gives to Kent; the wheel of impenetrable Fortune; the "sacred radiance of the sun"; and the macrocosm of fixed stars, remoter "orbs / From whom we do exist and cease to be" (1.1.110–11).

The most abstract of the play's circular images, as noted earlier, is the cipher zero. Paradoxically, the "naught" signifies both emptiness and fullness, absence of quantity and potential presence. We are introduced to its most negative aspect when the Fool calls his master "an O without a figure." But the "algorist" notion of zero as a "holding place" strengthens the positive aspects of circularity in the plot. The algorist zero came into Western mathematics with the Hindu-Arabic numerals and a decimal positional system, displacing the Roman system of numerals and dispensing with the need for an abacus to do quick calculations. For several centuries, there was keen competition between the "abacists," who manipulated an abacus for practical business purposes, and the "algorists" who used the new decimal arithmetic. (A sixteenth-century woodcut entitled *Margarita Philosophica* shows Dame Arithmetic

Margarita Philosophica (Freiburg, 1503). Arithmetic is instructing the algorist and the abacist. Woodcut from Gregor Reisch.

instructing the algorist on her right and the abacist on her left.) This algorist use of the "naught" as zero, which first entered English schoolbooks during Shakespeare's boyhood, projects a more complex—and far more benign—concept of "nothing" than the notion of mere absence or nullity. It is, in fact, the agent that permits the substitution of presence for absence, of value for null-value, just as the zero in the "tens" or center column of the number 103, for example, has no numerical value in itself but *holds the place open* for a digit that does have numerical value.

The mathematical use of zero as a holding place relates to the theme of presence-in-absence that runs like a silver thread through the whole action of *King Lear*. It explains the peculiar economy of the Fool/Cordelia exchange (including the practice in Shakespeare's time of both parts being played by the same actor). The place that is vacated by Cordelia is filled immediately by the Fool, and when Cordelia returns the Fool disappears. As Lear mourns Cordelia's death by crying "my poor fool is hanged!" we cannot help but mark the correspondence, whether we watch the performance or read the play. As William Empson noted with some vigor in his remarkable study of the Fool in *Lear*, "[T]he point is not that they are alike—it is shocking because they are so unalike—but that he must be utterly crazy to call one by the name of the other."[14] And so he must be, but his creator is not.

Shakespeare is linking these "unalike" characters at the simplest level by the mechanism of their interchangeability on stage. Just so, the algorist's zero is the mechanism of interchange. It betokens nonentity and potential identity. It signifies nothing, yet holds open the place for an entity shockingly unlike itself, a digit that "means something," a digit with a positive value that can take its place. Is it possible that Shakespeare is playfully manipulating the newest method of accounting here? That he has absorbed an exciting new mathematical concept of "nothing" and bent it to use on the stage of the Globe?

The round cipher that signifies the potential for presence, as well as unequivocal absence, may have a bearing on the more obvious relation of insight to blindness in the roles of both Lear and Gloucester. Gloucester perceives the truth only after he is literally blinded; he "sees" his own ignorance and the dark motives of those he trusted. That is, potential understanding becomes actual within the frame of literal darkness. Lear, "blinded" to the facts at first, similarly sees it all when reduced by Regan and Goneril to "an O without a figure." These refractions of the algorist zero into the very structure of the plot, taken together with the formal counterpoint of the "disquantity" passage and the Fool/Cordelia exchange, urge a reconsideration of Shakespeare's use of number—not in terms of mystical symbolism, but as a practical, living component of dramatic language.

By way of contrast, and to supply necessary background, I would like to draw attention to a fairly recent study of *King Lear* by a British scholar whose training is in mathematics. In *Signifying Nothing: The Semiotics of Zero*, Brian Rotman is chiefly interested in showing the relation between three "meta-signs": the zero as an indicator of absence, the "vanishing point" in perspective studies, and "xenomoney," or currency issued on paper. He is not interested in the zero as an instrument of potential presence, nor in exploring its ability to project ambivalent meanings. Rotman cleanly discriminates, however, between simple iterative counting and the use of number in more sophisticated mathematics. He traces the entrance of zero into European systems of computation and is able to suggest Shakespeare's probable training in elementary mathematics and accounting—extremely helpful information in the context of this study. Both Shakespeare and Ben Jonson, he points out, "were in the first generation of children in England to have learned about zero from Robert Recorde's Arithmetic, which bases itself on a strange pedagogical mixture of the new decimal notation and the old abacus manipulations."[15]

In his approach to *King Lear*, however, Rotman pursues a single-level "semiotics" reading of the zero as the evil genius of negation—Albany's "Most monstrous! O!" In Rotman's view, the drama "not only explicitly and obviously concerns itself with a certain sort of horror that comes from nothing, but less obviously . . . locates the origin of this horror in the secular effects and mercantile purport of the sign zero."[16] Rotman's reading of the "disquantity" passage stops short of Lear's "O!" From Regan's "What need one?" Rotman *deduces* that the king "arrives at zero" and, he concludes, "the language of arithmetic, in which the Fool articulates the loss of Lear's kinghood as the thing reduced to zero, becomes the vehicle and image of the destruction of Lear's self and natural love."[17] While Rotman rightly underscores the horror of vacuum in this reading, such an emphasis demands the most unambivalent interpretation of the zero figure possible, and possibly the least interesting. On the other hand, Rotman's juxtaposition of secular and emotional "currencies" is wonderfully valid for Lear, who, in not-so-sweet sessions of remembrance, will "heavily from woe to woe tell o'er / The sad account of fore-bemoanèd moan."

The point to be made is that the "destruction of Lear's self" and the loss of Regan and Goneril's "natural love"—that is, the loss of something less than genuine, of *arrogations* of love, unexamined assumptions about identity, unfounded assumptions about power—do indeed produce for Lear the empty space. But it is precisely in this vacuum that something positive develops. It is almost a critical cliché to observe that only in the space emptied of egocentric delusion is the devastated king able to recognize the value of Cordelia's love; where he acquires a sense of common humanity, the tenderness he extends to poor Tom, the humility he will bring to Cordelia. This is not to argue that *Lear* is a redemptive morality play—Elton's groundbreaking skeptical reading has corrected that misconception—but to comprehend that the circle of zero in it signifies something far more complex than Rotman's "ur-mark of absence." It is to see that the empty space in *Lear* is nothing less than a locus of transformation.

Clearly a single-level semiotics reading fails to register the complexity of the "conceit" determining the play's circular images, nor can it capture its pervasive ambivalence—an ambivalence that has marked also the reception of the zero since its first appearance in Western systems of accounting.[18] This is hardly the place to survey in detail the progress of the cipher from Hindu to Arabic mathematics, through its induction into thirteenth-century Europe by Fibonacci and his less brilliant, perhaps, but far more mysterious contemporary, Jordanus Nemorarius (*nemo*, Latin for "no man," "no one," "nobody"), until it jumps into the occupancy of the "empty set" some six hundred years later. We can note in passing that Gottlob Frege, in *The Foundations of Arithmetic* (1884), continued the cipher's history of ambivalence. After observing that "the charm of arithmetic lies in its rationality," the great logician and mathematician embedded the science of number, charmingly, in a paradox—recursively founding the whole structure on the cipher.[19] To be precise, Frege famously defined zero as "the Number which belongs to the concept 'not identical with itself,'" remarking at the same time that "some may find it shocking." He then defined one (1) as that number which belongs to the concept "identical with zero,"[20] thus continuing in the nineteenth century the contradictory status that the zero had traditionally enjoyed in Western thought. For centuries, Christian theology stood in conflict with pagan philosophy on this issue. The theological doctrine that God's Word created all that exists ex nihilo stood in sharp contradiction to the widespread classical principle: *ex nihilo nihil fit*, or, as Lear tells Cordelia, "Nothing will come of nothing."

The complex character of the figure "O," which is also the negative "O without a figure," can shed light on both the positive and negative circularities in *Lear*. Cordelia's ring, the play's manifest token of presence-in-absence, suggests both positive and negative possibilities. As a device, it serves to establish Kent's true identity and Cordelia's absolute integrity. It is the agent that summons her physical return to the stage, to the forefront of action and her father's side—but also to her undoing. The ring that symbolizes unity and fidelity also predicts the shape of the hangman's noose; the cord of filial attachment will lengthen into the swinging rope of death. Similarly, in the first act the sphere of light invoked by the king—the "sacred radiance of the sun"—is immediately balanced by his antithetical call to the "mysteries of Hecate and the night," suggestive of the new moon, the vacant round of blackness, the worship of dark forces (1.1.108–9). Finally, the wheel of blind Fortune that has stripped Lear of his powers turns on his enemies as well. As the bastard Edmund tells his vindicated brother: "The wheel is come full circle" (5.3.173).

We are returned at the last to the great "orbs" of the first act "from whom we do exist and cease to be." One feels shaken at the close of a performance of *King Lear*. One feels, like Prospero at the end of *The Tempest*, that the theater of action, "the great globe itself, / Yea, and all which it inherit, shall dissolve." And yet, one leaves the Globe Theatre after the show and walks out into another, larger world. The "orbs" in *King Lear* seem also to exist "outside the action" proper, as the remotest principles of causation. Perhaps they reflect a Lucretian nature of things, a pagan philosophy of impersonal divinities. Or perhaps they suggest the remarkable geometric notion of godhood that Jorge Luis Borges traced all the way from the pre-Socratics in his wonderful essay, "The Fearful Sphere of Pascal."[21] In the mid-sixteenth century, not long before the birth of the English bard, the French physician Rabelais was one of those who framed the idea anew, putting the words into the mouth of his sibylline priestess: "God is like an intelligible sphere whose center is everywhere and whose circumference is nowhere."

In the final scene of *Lear*, when the old order is gone, when the howls, the despair, and the suffering give place to silence, the remoter powers and greater cycles remain in force. In the face of apocalypse the remaining actors stir with activity; they are preparing to leave the stage, to vacate the set, to reduce the number (with good reason) to naught. The drama of the improvident old king comes to an end at ground zero, but it is surprisingly fertile ground. Some sixty years after the first printing of *Lear* in 1608, it was given to another surpassingly gifted poet to conceive an order of negation beyond the zero. The young Milton's sonnet *On Shakespear* celebrates the master's immortality in geometric images:

> What needs my *Shakespear* for his honor'd Bones
> The labour of an age in piled stones,
> Or that his hallow'd reliques should be hid
> Under a Star-ypointing *Pyramid?*

It remained for an older Milton bereft of external vision to travel beyond the zero, to reverse the "Star-ypointing *Pyramid*," to invent the epic mathematics of Pandaemonium, as we shall see in the chapter ahead.

3

The Mathematics of
Pandaemonium

The fall of the Rebel Angel in book 1 of *Paradise Lost*, and the conversion of his warriors from heavenly beings to an insectlike horde of demons, is told both by word and by number. Milton's narrative is supported by a mathematical "argument" whose elements are introduced within the first one hundred lines of verse, and further developed by figure, ratio, and image in the book's epic similes. That is to say, much of the story told by number and geometric figuration exists in a classical space—the space of the rhetorical trope, the extended analogy, the mathematical proportion conveyed by contrasting images.

Milton uses number and measure as a composer does, to provide an anchoring structure for flights of ornamented, melodic verse—but also as a logician, to securely ground the meanings generated by intricate turns of syntax. Perhaps the best indication we have of such a predisposition is the poet's declaration, directly prior to the Argument of book 1, that the verse of *Paradise Lost* will be constrained, not by any "jingling" rhyme scheme, but rather by number, measure, and internal logic. For "true musical delight," he notes, "consists in apt Numbers, fit quantity of Syllables, and the sense variously drawn out from one verse into another."[1] Clearly, the poet's "Numbers" here refers not to digits but to finely tuned meter. In book 1, however, he has chosen extremely apt numbers, qua number—the zero and the one—to structure the narrative of the infernal Seducer, once sublime, in a most adventurous way. And Milton has boldly introduced the newest physics and mathematics of his time into *Paradise Lost*: his fallen angel is deliberately subjected to a Galilean dynamics of motion (the heretical new physics) and the calculus of infinitesimals (the heretical new mathematics) after the Fall. Before turning to the extraordinary orchestration of

49

M. C. Escher. *Circle Limit IV.* Woodcut, 1960.
© 1996 M. C. Escher
Cordon Art—Baarn—Holland. All rights reserved.

these elements in the language of book 1, however, we need briefly to consider the sort of critical approach that deals with significant number.

ELIZABETHAN NUMBERS

There are two main approaches to a poet's use of number. One method is to apply a ready-made numerological system (Pythagorean, cabalistic, astrological, doctrinal) to specific digits and combinations of digits or number words as they occur in the text. The second approach seeks to isolate patterns and symmetries that shape the work as a whole. At times, the two methods overlap; Dante responds to both approaches, as does Milton's English predecessor, Spenser. One cannot read Dante fully without some idea of his numerology—the astrological relationships and theological doctrine (chiefly that of Aquinas) that determine the various number choices of the *Commedia*, the famous "nines" of the *Vita Nuova*. Spenser, on the other hand, gravitates away from Catholic symbolism and toward Neoplatonic numerology, as has been definitively established. And while Milton clearly valued Dante,[2] in the *Areopagitica* he distances himself even further from Roman Catholicism when he calls the "sage and serious Spenser" a better teacher than Aquinas.

Critical analyses of Elizabethan numerology have drawn upon widely known works such as Vincent Hopper's *Medieval Number Symbolism* (1938), Rudolph Wittkower's study of Pythagorean proportion in his *Architectural Principles in the Age of Humanism* (1965), and the occult symbology set forth by Frances Yates in her fine study, *Giordano Bruno and the Hermetic Tradition* (1964). As far back as 1925, Denis Saurat explored Milton's connection with the *Zohar* and the cabalistic science of number; more recent studies include C. A. Patrides' "Numerological approach to Cosmic Order during the English Renaissance" (1958) and Maren-Sofie Røstvig's *The Hidden Sense: Milton and the Neoplatonic Method of Numerical Composition* (1963), an examination of patterns and symmetries in Milton's poetry that suggest, as she believes, theological and philosophical parallels. Most notably, A. Kent Heiatt's study, *Short Time's Endless Moment: The Symbolism of the Numbers in Edmund Spenser's "Epithalamion"* (1960), initiated a number of serious critical analyses, including Alastair Fowler's lucid *Spenser and the Numbers of Time* (1964) and his later work *Triumphal Forms: Structural Patterns in Elizabethan Poetry* (1970).[3]

Most of the elements of medieval numerology are woven into Spenser's *Faerie Queene*, according to Fowler. "Pythagorean number symbolism, astronomical symbolism based on orbital figures and on Ptolemaic star catalogue totals, [and] medieval theological number symbolism" systematically structure the narrative, he points out, and "all of these strands . . . are worked into what must be one of the most intricate poetic textures ever devised."[4] We see an example of this intricate texture in Spenser's description of the castle of Alma:

> The frame thereof seemed partly circulare,
> And part triangulare: O worke divine!
> Those two the first and last proportions are;
> The one imperfect, mortall, foemenine,
> Th' other immortall, perfect, masculine:
> And twixt them both a quadrate was the base,
> Proportioned equally by seven and nine;
> Nine was the circle sett in heaven's place;
> All which compacted made a goodly diapase.
>
> (2.9.22)[5]

Besides the mathematical relations indicated by the terms "proportioned" and "equally," the stanza contains Euclidean figures of the circle, triangle, and square, the numerals *two, one, seven, nine*—and the freestanding "O," which simulates the cipher. All these elements are amenable to occult interpretation of the sort categorized by Fowler; indeed, the stanza almost seductively invites numerological readings of the magical kind. As we shall shortly see, however, a more rational point of view, closer perhaps to Milton's own perception, had begun to develop well before Spenser.

The second approach to mathematical symbolism reveals numerical patterns governing large and small segments of a work, but is also concerned to demonstrate mythic resonances and philosophical attitudes encoded in its geometric images. An instance of methodological overlap (i.e., using both approaches) occurs in Fowler's *Triumphal Forms*. This passage, worth quoting at some length, connects Copernican heliocentric physics with the sun imagery of *Paradise Lost* and emphasizes at the same time that Milton is drawing upon *both* the Ptolemaic and Copernican systems. Here Fowler posits a rich interweaving of political, Hermetic, and mythic elements with scientific theory: "The success of the Copernican theory led to a single indubitable centre, more emphatic than that of the Ptolemaic system. . . . Pythagorean and Neoplatonic solar theory enjoyed a revival, and the 'Orphic' solar mysticism . . . [was] illustrated by Apollo *in mezzo delle Muse* [in the midst of the

Muses] because his light informs all men's intellectual activities." In the baroque style, Fowler continues, "such ideas might be applied politically, as in the cult of the *Roi Soleil*. Alternatively, there was Milton's more abstract return to the geometrical mysticism of Cusanus and Ficino. Their Hermetic doctrine of God as simultaneous centre and circumference of the universal circle . . . underlies the strong emphasis on solar and divine centrality in *Paradise Lost*: 'as God in Heav'n / Is Center, yet extends to all'" (9.107–8).[6]

Milton complicates the issue, for he openly condemns magical number crunching in the prose, yet quietly employs number symbolism in the poetry. This makes sense if we recall that he is living at a time when the mystical aspects of number were being supplanted—or at least supplemented—by great advances in mathematics. It was a time when efforts were being made to understand the universe in terms of strict mathematical laws, as Paul Oscar Kristeller has observed, and when, in fact, the rational attitude toward geometry and number had been prepared by the very same Platonists cited by Fowler: Nicholas of Cusa and Marsilio Ficino. "Renaissance Platonists such as Cusanus and Ficino brought the notion of innate ideas and principles back into prominence," Kristeller points out, "and thus paved the way for the later rationalist position adopted by such thinkers as Descartes." He adds, "[T]he emphasis on the a priori certainty and perfection of mathematical knowledge . . . had a definite impact upon early modern physical science, as can be seen in the case of Galileo, and especially of Kepler."[7] These last two figures, of course, were Milton's contemporaries.

What must be underscored, here, is that the "rationalist" Galileo—mathematician, astronomer, and poet—is the single *historical* figure other than Columbus to appear in the twelve books of *Paradise Lost*. He is uniquely contemporary. Milton refers to him in three separate books (books 1, 3, and 5), always as part of a simile. He is *named* the third time as a shadowy parallel to Raphael, the messenger archangel, who sees across the cosmos with unobstructed vision,

> As when by night the Glass
> Of *Galileo*, less assur'd, observes
> Imagind Lands and Regions in the Moon.
>
> (5.261–63)

But there are persuasive indications of Milton's ardently rational mind-set, other than a *Zeitgeist* dedicated to intellectual activity on all fronts. Three come easily to mind: (1) the young man's explicit interest in keeping abreast of the latest developments in mathematics and his subsequent ability to tutor his students, not only in arithmetic and geometry but also in "analytics" (algebra), trigonometry, and what he refers to as the *canon Logarithmicum*, or logarithms;[8] (2) Milton's espousal of Ramist logic, documented by his 1672 treatise on the subject *(Artis Logicae Plenior Institutio)*;[9] and (3) his desire to separate the theology of *Paradise Lost* as much as possible from Roman trappings, including numerology. It is, in fact, in the treatise on Christian doctrine that one finds Milton placing strict emphasis on the plain, Protestant sense of number, first in a treatment of the unity of God and again, as Røstvig has noted, in a discussion of the Sabbath.[10]

In his discussion of the nature of God, in book 1 of *Christian Doctrine* (*Joannis Miltoni Angli De Doctrina Christiana*, translated and published posthumously in 1825), Milton immediately underscores the ordinary, pedestrian sense of the singular numeral. After enumerating eight of the nine attributes of the Deity, he names the final attribute: "that God is ONE, proceeds from the eight previous attributes and is, as it were, the logical conclusion of them all." He then observes, in a tone almost ingenuous in its simple rationality,

> What could be better adapted to the average intelligence, what more in keeping with everyday speech, so that God's people should understand that there is numerically one God and one Spirit, just as they understand that there is numerically one of anything else.[11]

In the seventh book of the same work, as Røstvig and other numerological readers have somewhat reluctantly noted, Milton argues against "mere number" possessing magical properties or mystical value in itself. It is up to his opponents, he claims, to prove "what moral value there can possibly be in the number seven. It is up to them to show us why, released from Sabbath observation, we should still be bound by a seven—*by a mere numeral, without force or efficacy*" (my emphasis).[12] Clearly, the thrust here is toward demystification. These statements should not be shrugged off as anomalies, but given serious consideration in any treatment of number in Milton's works.

Zero/Shield and One/Spear

We can now investigate Milton's treatment of the two salient numbers in book 1 of *Paradise Lost*, not as instances of mystical numerology but as brilliantly deployed tactical agents. The *zero* and the *one* can be seen as mathematical objects intrinsic to the exposition and as literary *figurae*, drawing upon Erich Auerbach's complex sense of the term.[13] That is, zero and one can be understood as highly resonant symbols, subject to a family of related interpretations, that yet retain a root meaning and their defining shape. These *figurae* occur together, always paired—*circle* and *vertical line*—appearing variously as Homeric weapons, gender symbols, geometric figures, celestial orbs and trails, and as the primary digits indicated by number words in the text—from Greek *myriad* (ten thousand) to the infinitesimal calculus of the seventeenth century.

As conjoined mathematical and figural objects, the paired numbers establish a metanarrative. In book 1, they can be shown to mimetically parallel the series of radical changes that transforms Satan into the very principle of mutability and reduces his host from infinite angelic beings to a swarm of virtually "numberless" infinitesimals. It falls to the zero and one—in that order—to function in this book as agents of inconstancy and ambivalence *in direct contrast to the readings prescribed by mystical numerology for the circle and the unity*.

We will turn, directly, to the passage in book 1 where both the circle and the line are enlarged to titanic proportions. One must keep in mind, however, that Milton has introduced the mathematical elements of *Paradise Lost* within the poem's first eighty lines of verse. Within this frame he sets the first *equation*: "He [Satan] trusted to have equal'd the most High" (line 40); the first *cardinal number* and the first *multiplication*: "Nine times the space that measures Day and Night" (line 50); and the first pairing of circle and line, as Satan takes in his surroundings, in a way that joins geometry to number, as a circumference followed by the number word "one": "A Dungeon horrible, *on all sides round* / As *one* great Furnace flam'd" (lines 61–62; my emphasis). These mathematical elements occur at ten-line intervals, and the first *ratio* appears some ten lines further. The nethermost prison that is hell and "darkness visible" lies at a measured distance:

> As far remov'd from God and light of Heav'n
> As from the Center to th' utmost Pole.
>
> (lines 73–74)

While "Center" and "Pole" suggest the span to the primum mobile, or outermost Ptolemaic sphere, they also serve to repeat the *figurae* of circle and line. Finally, the first *ordinal number* appears at the opening of, appropriately, the second verse paragraph and establishes the prime element of a series. That is, the repeated ordinals, "Say *first* . . . say *first*" (lines 27–28) calling upon the Muse to speak, or to speak ordinally through the poet, are followed by "One *next* . . . and *next*" (line 79), the recognition of Beelzebub that prompts Satan's first speech. Numerical series are made possible only through the incremental repetition of identical quantities. Thus, the *systematic repetition of an identical term* suggests a numerical series (first . . . next) as much as it contributes to narrative continuity, or indicates the hierarchical status of Satan and Beelzebub.

The celebrated "Galileo" passage of book 1 describes the arms of the "superiour Fiend" as he moves from the burning lake to the burning shore. Milton gives us first the archangelic shield, of a magnitude and mass far greater than the epic shield of Achilles, which represents the world in microcosm and was also forged by a divine smith. The satanic shield in Milton's epic is lunar, thus symbolically "foeminine" and "imperfect":

> . . . his ponderous shield
> Ethereal temper, massy, large and round,
> Behind him cast; the broad circumference
> Hung on his shoulders like the Moon, whose Orb
> Through Optic Glass the *Tuscan* Artist views
> At Ev'ning from the top of *Fesole*,
> Or in *Valdarno*, to descry new Lands,
> Rivers or Mountains in her spotty Globe.
>
> (lines 284–91)

We see the shield's "broad circumference" transferred first to the disk of the full moon, then miniaturized in the optic lens, and continually refracted in the host of upper- and lowercase *o*'s distributed throughout the passage. The newly discovered phenomenon of the moon's actual sphericality is reflected first in the "Orb" of the moon, then in small in the unseen eye of the scientist who "views," and is then transferred once more to the orbiting "Globe" he is observing. Satan's shield grows geometrically solid in the images of "Orb" and "Globe," but Milton brings the plane and solid figures together in the "spotty" lunar landscape, spotted with "seas" and craters. These are the geometric forms one sees at a great distance: round disks inscribed upon a sphere.

While the triumph of Galileo's natural philosophy is apparent in the newly magnified lunar surface, "spotty" is not a noble attribute. It suggests the pox; it suggests the "imperfect" feminine; above all, it suggests the darker sublunary aspect of the physics that unfixed the divine order of the cosmos. At the same time, the circles and spheres generated by the trope of the Moon, with its two o's—or empty eyes?—are all of them signatures of the zero. Like the moon, an empty circle of darkness when "new" that by measured degrees attains to fullness and *reflected* light, the zero—as noted in an earlier chapter—is a circle empty of value in itself but also an entity that holds open the place for potential value and fullness. In Milton's time, the moon has become a wonder and a source of theological conflict, the direct result of Galileo's discoveries. The zero is still an ambivalent algorithmic monster. These resonances are calculated to give the Galileo simile its satanic cast.

It seems reasonably evident that Milton is gravitating between mythic and historic time, in *Paradise Lost*. From the outset, he weaves Homeric weapons and Hesiodic wars together with Christian theology and the latest developments in mathematics and astronomy. The narrative layering is reminiscent of Dante's fourfold dimensionality. The passage we have been looking at, however, is remarkable in that it preempts modern camera techniques with a dazzling *sprezzatura* (to use Stanley Fish's term). The perspective "zooms in" from the distant orb of the moon right down along the plane of the telescope itself; it moves past the lens to the "orb" of the viewer, and then travels back out again for a "long shot" of the spotty globe. It is as though the poet kept reversing the instrument of cosmic observation, looking first through one end of the telescope and then through the other—with a single Cyclopean eye. This seeing Center now fastens upon Satan's spear which, in a manner of speaking, becomes a kind of "utmost Pole."

Stanley Fish has argued persuasively that the passage describing the spear leads us to distrust our perceptions. It accomplishes instantaneous and deceitful changes in size, he holds, because of the simile's ambiguous syntax, while the time lag caused by having to readjust to the *sense* of the imagery perplexes the understanding and dislocates the reader. "Where are we, what are the physical components of our surroundings, what time is it?" asks Fish.[14] He is right, of course. The Galileo passage deliberately calls both visual perception and mental grasp into question. It would seem that Milton is confronting the relative nature of *physical* reality at this point, at a time of catastrophic change—equivalent to the move in our own time from classical to quantum physics.

We can assume that the archangelic spear was also forged in heaven, and that its size is commensurate with that of the shield. That is, we can expect the Rebel Angel to carry a spear that "goes with" a shield the size of the moon. We are given an idea of his magnitude by the description of him as he lies chained on the burning lake: "many a rood, in bulk as huge / As whom the Fables name of monstrous size" (1.196–97). A *rood* is 3,630 square feet: one-quarter of an acre.[15] This titanic figure, as we know, will undergo metamorphoses and extreme reductions in physical mass, as when he takes the shape of a toad or serpent. Similarly, Satan's spear—i.e., the "male " member of the paired *figurae*—even more insistently than the circular shield, appears to undergo astonishing fluctuations in size:

> His Spear, to equal which the tallest Pine
> Hewn on *Norwegian* hills, to be a Mast
> Of some great Ammiral, were but a wand,
> He walkt with to support uneasie steps. . . .
>
> (lines 292–95)

Milton has framed this sequence as a mathematical proportion ($A : B :: C : D$) so that we rightly anticipate logical relationships. But the "given" is a series of images, all linear, all vertically erect, that suggest a reduction in magnitude from the godlike to the heroic to something crippled. And while the middle terms of the proportion are easy to envision (spear is to pine as pine is to wand)[16] the outer terms escape measure. They cannot be pinned down. If we knew the length of the "wand" we could perhaps work out the dimensions of the spear—but we do not know. Fish thinks that Milton is generating "the awe that attends incomprehensibility" and half-jokingly comments on the inadequacy of the ratio: "I submit that any attempt either to search out masts of Norwegian ships or to determine the mean length of wands is irrelevant."[17]

Although we cannot know its "mean length," Milton's choice of the term "wand" is anything but irrelevant. What we do know is that Satan is using it to help himself move through the waters of "that inflamed sea" (line 300). Is it an allusion to Aaron's rod, as Linda Gregerson suggests, summoning up biblical plagues such as frogs and locusts? "As a magic rod, the wand has precedents. . . . Moses perplexes Pharaoh with his 'wand.'"[18] Or does the wand of the magician in Milton's *Comus*—a baton with the power to paralyze and "enchain"—lend meaning to Satan's wand? Gregerson concludes with justice that "a wand is more than a negligible item, even when compared to a pine tree or to Satan's spear."

I would like to suggest that Milton has chosen the term "wand," at least in part, because it sounds so much like the word "one." If this is so, then the underlying logic of Milton's proportion becomes intelligible. For the one/wand can magically replicate itself $(1 + 1 + 1 + 1 \ldots)$ to "many a rood" and *continue to mathematical infinity*. It thus preserves a symmetry of infinite extremes in a fluctuating "incomprehensible" ratio. At the same time, and this is the central point, it discloses the singular *figura* that generates the Galileo simile's *linear* images—including the telescope itself, as well as the spear, pine tree, mast, and wand. The trope of the wand conveys number magic indeed, but a magic that most logically and most precisely suggests the infinite dimensions of the ethereal spear.

The great shield and spear of the Galileo passage can be understood, then, as macrocosmic representations of an ur-shape. The forms appear first as archaic instruments of war. As the "spotty Globe" of the moon and the "Mast / Of some great Ammiral" they signify sexual archetypes, if the Freudian distinction holds. Certainly they convey abstract Euclidean forms, both plane and solid. As numbers, the zero and one hugely represent the Nothing and the Something, which, in its theological symbolism, becomes the "brooding on the abyss" that brings forth creation. This whole "family" of individual forms, in *Paradise Lost*, may be derived from the original *figurae*, the Platonic intuitions, so to speak, of zero and one.

Concerning Two New Sciences

It is worth taking a moment to consider why Milton, composing an epic about the Fall, should select Galileo as one of its dramatis personae. As noted earlier, the Pisan astronomer is the only contemporary figure to be named in *Paradise Lost*. It is significant that Milton pays tribute from the very beginning of his poem to a man who had contributed greatly to a rational new vision of the cosmos. Perhaps equally meaningful to the poet, Galileo had suffered ecclesiastical trial and condemnation for rejecting a Catholic worldview and for furthering Copernican physics. On his European tour (1638–39),the thirty-year-old Milton made a trip to Pisa, Galileo's birthplace—and the scene of his experiments concerning the momentum of falling objects.[19] In *Areopagitica* (1644), perhaps the most powerful condemnation of censorship ever written, Milton recorded his visit with Galileo in the Tuscan hills: "There it was that I found and visited the famous *Galileo* grown old, a prisoner of the Inquisition, for thinking in Astronomy otherwise than the Franciscan and Dominican licencers thought."[20]

Galileo had proposed radical theories of motion. He had measured the height of mountains on the moon. He posited a universe comprehensible by mathematical concepts alone: "Philosophy is written in that great book which ever lies before our eyes—I mean the universe—but this book," he warns, "is written *in the mathematical language and the symbols are triangles, circles, and other geometrical figures, without whose help it is impossible to comprehend a single word of it; without which one wanders in a dark labyrinth.*"[21] One historian of science reminds us that to appreciate the full import of Galileo's discoveries, "we must understand the importance of abstract thinking, of its use by Galileo as a . . . more revolutionary instrument than even the telescope."[22] While the poet of *Paradise Lost* was consigned to physical darkness, with "wisdom at one entrance quite shut out," his surpassing gift was to see and tell of "things invisible to mortal sight." Like Galileo, he was at home in the realm of abstract thought, of imaginative flight. And he was certainly conversant with the language of mathematics.

There is evidence that from his student days onward, Milton was deeply interested in the rapidly developing mathematical concepts of his time, "some of them . . . advanced and abstruse," as H. F. Fletcher comments in his study of Milton's intellectual development.[23] We know too, from the *Second Defense* (1654), that during the period Milton spent at Hammersmith and Horton after receiving his advanced degree from Cambridge (1632–38), his only break from self-imposed studies were trips into London "to learn what was new in mathematics and music, then the objects of [his] special studies" (8:120–21). Just at this time, groundbreaking discoveries in mathematics and physics were preparing the way for Newton and a mathematically describable universe. Certain of these radical new theories found their way into Milton's all-encompassing poem.

What was "new in mathematics" was part of an unparalleled explosion in scientific thought, both on the Continent and in England. This was the era of Descartes, Fermat, Pascal, Huygens, and John Wallis. By 1629, while Milton was still at Cambridge, Pierre Fermat's studies of loci and curves (*The Method of Maxima and Minima*) was circulating via other mathematicians in France and Italy. Fermat, a lawyer and brilliant amateur of mathematics, is credited not only with cofounding analytic geometry with Descartes, but is recognized also as a source of modern number theory and the discoverer of the differential calculus. His process of "changing the variable slightly and considering neighboring values has ever since been the essence of infinitesimal calculus," according to historian Carl B. Boyer.[24] Fermat also devised a method of proving theorems by a species of mathematical induction, which can be used to reveal false premises; he christened it "infinite descent."[25] In his comprehensive survey of the mathematical thought of the period, the philosopher of science D. T. Whiteside points out that concepts of "number, space, and limit . . . were the keystone of the immense proliferation of mathematical discoveries during the 17th century."[26] It is precisely the newly-invented infinitesimal calculus that concerns us here, as well as the notion of "infinite descent"—a fit mathematics, it would seem, for the denizens of Pandaemonium.

Somewhat earlier, in 1619, Johann Kepler had dedicated his *Harmonices Mundi*—a mystical conglomeration of astronomy, music, and mathematics—to James I, which gained him an invitation to the English court. In 1631 in England, Harriot published an algebra, *Artis Analyticae Praxis*, and Oughtred the *Clavis Mathematicae* (Key to mathematics). Between 1632 and 1638 alone, the crucial period when Milton was heading into London to search out the latest developments, there were such publications as Cavalieri's *Geometria Indivisibilibus* (which included some of Fermat's new ideas); Descartes's enormously influential *Discours de la méthode* (1637), with the three books of the *Géométrie* appended (an application of algebra to geometry and geometry to algebra, as Boyer notes); and Galileo's last, and some think best, work: *Discourses and Demonstrations Concerning Two New Sciences* (1638). In the spring of that same year, Milton set off for an extended tour of France and Italy and sought out "the famous *Galileo*."

Closer to home was John Wallis (1616–1703), who invented the "love-knot" symbol for infinity in use today. In 1655, some twelve years before the publication of *Paradise Lost*, Wallis brought out the *Arithmetica Infinitorum* which, as Boyer tells us, "arithmetisized the *Geometria indivisibilibus* of Cavalieri."[27] Wallis's *Arithmetica* was the immediate influence that "precipitated Newton's considerations a decade later," as Edna E. Kramer notes.[28] Along with Leibnitz's work, Newton's "considerations" brought about a prodigious leap in mathematics, the science of calculus, which for the first time permitted the *mathematical analysis of all movement and change*. By the years 1665 and 1666—that is, just one year before the publication of *Paradise Lost*—Newton had devised "a marvelously automatic mental tool for operating on an equation in order to get at infinitesimals."[29] Newton's calculus may have remained unpublished for nearly forty years, but the finest mathematical minds of the time were seriously engaged with problems of motion, on the one hand, and the rigorous description of infinitudes and infinitesimals, on the other. In this context, Milton's countryman and contemporary, John Wallis, deserves particular notice.

Wallis held the chair of mathematics at Oxford for fifty-four years, spanning the interregnum, and though he appears to have been a known Royalist, we learn that "the regime of Cromwell was not averse to using his services in the deciphering of secret codes."[30] Evidently his passion for problem solving transcended whatever political objections he may have had. One can but conjecture as to whether the paths of John Wallis, Savilian Professor of Geometry, and John Milton, Secretary for Foreign Tongues, crossed during the ten years that Milton served the Commonwealth (1649–59). We do know, however, that in 1655, during Milton's tenure as secretary, Wallis published two "very important books, one in analytical geometry, the other in infinite analysis . . . the two leading branches of mathematics at the time." Specifically, we find that Wallis *replaced geometrical concepts by numerical ones whenever possible*: "Even proportion, the stronghold of ancient geometry, Wallis held to be an arithmetic concept."[31]

The trend in seventeenth-century mathematics that began to penetrate geometry with "analytics" or algebra, and to supplant Euclidean figures with numerical operations, generated the first studies since Zeno of mathematical infinitudes. These historic developments are reflected in the mathematical structures of *Paradise Lost*. What can be shown most clearly, perhaps, is the explicit *mathematical* structuring of Pandaemonium, where Milton parallels the historic convergence of geometry with number as the action of book 1 approaches its climax.

THE "FABRICK HUGE" OF ANTISPACE

Book 1, as Milton tells us in the Argument, proposes "in brief, the whole Subject." We can now approach those episodes that, with the "Galileo" passage, best reveal its mathematical "argument": the marching Phalanx; the Dorian mode; the dimming of Lucifer as a division by halves; the archangel's descent and the dynamics of falling objects; demonic operations with negative number; and the climactic introduction of infinitesimals into Pandaemonium, making the domain of Lucifer a virtual antispace. All these episodes are linked together by the presence of the key *figurae.*

Following the parade of pagan deities, Satan's standard is unfurled to the blare of horns. A rich tapestry of sound and color and unceasing motion evokes the splendor of a royal progress. As the scene takes shape, geometric figures are seen to solidify and condense. Satan's legions become squared and cubed as they assemble "in perfect *Phalanx*," while the depth of the formation is "immeasurable":

> Ten thousand Banners rise into the Air
> With Orient Colours waving: with them rose
> A Forrest huge of Spears: and thronging Helms
> Appear'd, and serried Shields in thick array
> Of depth immeasurable: Anon they move
> In perfect *Phalanx* to the *Dorian* mood
> Of Flutes and soft Recorders;
>
> (lines 545–51)

While the one and zero *figurae* are in high profile here, both as numerical quantities (ten thousand) and geometric shapes (spears and shields), we see that the proportions of the original shield and spear have diminished in size but increased greatly in number.

Milton's choice of *Phalanx* and *Dorian* mode, drawn from the Greek arts of war and music, respectively, lend strong support to the mathematical substructure of the passage. The music to which the Phalanx moves brings to the forefront a modal system that had undergone changes in number, character (from pitch to tonality), and hierarchy since classical antiquity. Aristotle, in the *Politics*, had upheld the Dorian as the "manliest" of the modes, which makes it a singularly appropriate accompaniment to the military formation.[32] Church music in Milton's time used fourteen tonal modes and over time had moved the Dorian from fourth to first place. Of the fourteen, the Dorian is the mode that appears most symmetrical in notation. The two halves of its octave are identical mirror images, for the semitones occur as intervals between the second and third notes, and again between the sixth and seventh notes of the scale. To those acquainted with the modes—that "fit audience though few"—the Dorian suggested graphic concepts of symmetry and equidistant halftones. Arthur E. Barker, surveying the structural patterns in *Paradise Lost*, asserts that, as a result of his blindness, "Milton's mind operated at ease only when he perceived in or imposed on his material a precise mathematical division of some sort."[33] This seems to hold true, particularly at this point, where Milton is preparing to introduce a series of "halfs" into the text—and so multiply his demon horde by fractionating it. In this respect, his choice of musical mode seems as perfectly designed as the military formation it accompanies.

The "perfect *Phalanx*" is a masterstroke. Milton first projects a solid figure, then deconstructs it as the passage unfolds, turning suddenly from geometry to number. In Homer, the "phalanx" refers to a single line of battle, although in later classical works it has come to mean a squared formation of heavily-armed infantry drawn up in close ranks, shields joined and spears overlapping. This human version of an armored tank composed "a compact mass of infantry usually of 8 deep, but also as much as 25 deep," according to Liddell and Scott's *Greek-English Lexicon*. In the seventeenth century, the phalanx was considered the ideal battle formation, Milton himself calling it "an embleme of truth and stedfastnesse" in the 1642 treatise on church government. In the passage under consideration, however, the geometry is deconstructed, so to speak; it breaks down into ever simpler components as we review the phalanx through Satan's eyes. It changes from a dense *solid* "Of depth immeasurable," to a *plane* figure, "a horrid Front / Of dreadful length," to a mere *line* of stick-figures, "armed Files," and is further reduced to a collection of *points* as Satan counts their *number*. Notably, the "bad angels" still possess godlike magnitude and beauty:

> Advanc't in view they stand, a horrid Front
> Of dreadful length and dazling Arms, in guise
> Of Warriers old with order'd Spear and Shield,
> Awaiting what command thir mighty Chief
> Had to impose: He through the armed Files
> Darts his experienc't eye, and soon traverse
> The whole Battalion views, thir order due,
> Thir visages and stature as of Gods
> Thir number last he sums.
>
> (lines 562–71)

The images of Satan's massive moon-shield and the limitless spear increasingly give way to numerical figures as the book nears its end: "Ten thousand Banners" (line 545), "Millions of spirits" (line 609), "hunderds and thousands" (line 760), and in the (ironic?) address, "O Myriads . . . O Powers" (line 622). (In context, "Powers" may refer to squared and cubed numbers as much as to a rank of angels.) The number words give an impression of countless multitudes, as they are meant to do, but they also reproduce in small the paired shapes of the *figurae*—with a reversal of order. In place of shield and spear we now have "one" and "zero," a few ones, and many, many zeros.

As the darkening archangel reflects upon the number of his host, the key shapes reoccur, this time in archetypal images of the Tower and the Sun-in-eclipse. Satan's loss of grace is exacerbated, in the passage below, by the contrast with the "Sun new ris'n," prefiguring the coming of Christ. The "Towr" is especially striking in context, not only as a "type" of Babel but as the scene of Galileo's earliest experiments in the dynamics of falling bodies. Milton isolates the fallen angel, at this moment verbally split in two as "Arch Angel" and visibly dimming:

> . . . he above the rest
> In shape and gesture proudly eminent
> Stood like a Towr; his form had not yet lost
> All her Original brightness, nor appear'd
> Less than Arch Angel ruind, and th' excess
> Of Glory obscur'd: As when the Sun new ris'n
> Looks through the Horizontal misty Air
> Shorn of his Beams, or from behind the Moon
> In dim Eclips disastrous twilight sheds
> On half the Nations, and with fear of change
> Perplexes Monarchs. Dark'n'd so, yet shon
> Above them all th' Arch Angel:
>
> (line 589–600)

Here begins the tale of "halfs," the series of divisions and doublings that will sharply accelerate as the action approaches its climax. Inevitably changing into the Prince of Darkness, the fallen angel is at this point only half transformed. We find "Archangel" twice split into "Arch Angel," a crafty way station on the road from good to bad. The sun in lunar eclipse indicates both a lessened and a doubled entity, while "disastrous twilight" means both "two-light" and the half light that occurs before total darkness. Although the ten thousand banners are now grown to "Millions of flaming swords" (664), the "halfs" continue to multiply: "*half* the Nations" are darkened in the simile of the eclipse; when Satan addresses the host, "thir *doubled* ranks they bend . . . and *half* enclose him round" (lines 616–17); he expresses contempt for the Opponent: "who overcomes / By force, hath overcome but *half* his foe" (lines 648–49).

The once-angelic host are also undergoing changes wrought by halving and doubling. They no longer possess "visages and stature as of Gods," but rather suddenly have become the three faceless multitudes that labor like worker bees to raise the "Fabrick huge" of Pandaemonium.

All the quantity terms now applied to these new inhabitants of hell suggest uncountable infinitudes; their number can no longer be "summed." Like the damned souls of the *Inferno*, or Virgil's twittering shades, they are *Thick as autumnal leaves, innumerable*, a *cloud / Of locusts, numberless . . . bad Angels*, a *hasty multitude*, a *promiscuous crowd*. They have *swarmed* and *throng numberless*. Satan's legions have become legion. At the last, they are said to be *without number*. Without number!

Following the construction of Pandaemonium, Time enters the poem. In the lines that so struck William Blake, Milton combines pagan and Hebrew myths of falling deities, the notion of a Sublime Architect cast down, Ptolemaic celestial spheres, and Kepler's crystalline music. At the same time he manages to suggest the new Galilean physics of acceleration. In spite of this heavy baggage, the fall of Lucifer is projected with great delicacy as a tale within a tale, with classical coloration and extraordinary purity of line:

> . . . thrown by angry *Jove*
> Sheer o're the Chrystal Battlements: from Morn
> To Noon he fell, from Noon to dewy Eve,
> A Summer's day; and with the setting Sun
> Dropt from the Zenith like a falling Star
>
> (lines 741–45)

The *figurae* in this passage are luminous and seemingly transcendent, but they introduce time and measured motion into the cosmic apparatus of the poem. The Sun, being swallowed by the Earth, is losing its sphericality; the Star is falling, which supplies a shining vertical—the fast-disappearing trace of the comet's "tail." It is the measured fall from the zenith, however, that hints at scientific studies of momentum, the rate of falling objects that Galileo described in terms of ratio, number, and squares of numbers.[34] Milton indicates his familiarity with the "Tuscan Artist's" formulations, first by selecting a ratio as his vehicle and then in measuring the Fall by diurnal motion—"from Morn / To Noon he fell, from Noon to dewy Eve." With the striking image of the falling star, a Galilean "per second per second" vector of acceleration pierces the space traveled by the cast-out-of-heaven Vulcan/Lucifer, and an action that until this moment has occurred outside measurable time suddenly takes on temporality. This plummeting descent out of mythic time and into Galilean space-time heralds the final catastrophic change.

As book 1 draws to a close, we see Satan's armies grow infinitely numerous as they crowd into an increasingly smaller area. The "squared Regiments" (line 758) that march into Pandaemonium become anonymous digits within the space of two lines of verse: "they anon / With hunderds and with thousands trooping came" (line 760), and continue to move relentlessly into what modern mathematical logic has casually referred to as a "contracted neighborhood."[35] They populate every inch of available space, "Thick swarm'd, both on the ground and in the air" (line 768) and continue to densify and compact until they are pressed and squeezed into one another. At the same time we learn that they have grown "airie": "So thick the aerie crowd / Swarm'd and were strait'n'd; till the Signal giv'n" (lines 775–76).

Satan's signal is powerful magic. It triggers an instantaneous crossover to a negative order of existence. They who were infinite are transformed into infinitesimals:

> Behold a wonder! they but now who seemd
> In bigness to surpass Earths Giant Sons
> Now less than smallest Dwarfs, in narrow room
> Throng numberless.
>
> (lines 777–80)

Geoffrey Hartmann has pointed out that Milton's finest effects derive from his similes of magnification and diminishment, and he observes justly that such tropes "not only magnify or diminish the doings in hell, but invariably put them at a distance."[36] Clearly, a "telescoping" has taken place at this critical juncture. Indeed, the "aerie crowd" (above) and the "incorporeal Spirits" (below) may be understood on one level to signify "abstract numbers."

Most striking of all, however, is the realization that Milton has dramatically conceived hell—like heaven—as a realm of logical paradox. If one accepts the oxymorons here as strategic and deliberate—"numberless" throngs; "Reduc't" shapes "at large"; numbers "without number"—then one discovers Zeno's mischievous paradoxes against motion made visible:

> Thus incorporeal Spirits to smallest forms
> Reduc't thir shapes immense, and were at large
> Though without number still amidst the Hall`
> Of that infernal Court.
>
> (lines 789–92)[37]

The term "still" is ambiguous in context, and may be read as "silent," "extant," or "motionless." There is, in fact, a full stop at this point; the great emigration has come to an end. Indeed, for the proletarian demon there seems small hope of getting anywhere. He has been "strait'n'd" by a convergent series $(1/2 + 1/4 + 1/8 + 1/16 \ldots)$ and arrived at a mathematical limit.[38]

Satan's chief lords, however, retain their former magnitude, although even these elite ones, seated in the Unholy of Unholies of that infernal edifice, are lessened by a final "halving" to *Demy*-powers:

> But far within
> And in thir own dimension like themselves
> The great Seraphic Lords and Cherubim
> In close recess and secret conclave sat
> A thousand Demy-gods on golden seats

(lines 792–96)

Most remarkably, one finds that a distortion of Euclidean space is made the stage for essential evil. While the great mass of fallen spirits—the fractionated immensities that seem as immaterial as "Faerie Elves"—are contained "in narrow room," the select figures of hell sit hugely enlarged, in proportion, but they too occupy an unnatural continuum. Milton has situated the malign powers in a disfigured space that corresponds to the minor demons' conversion to infinitesimals. Satan's conference chamber is a paradoxical *multum in parvo* where "far within" the great structure of Pandaemonium a thousand Demy-gods—the greater volume—sit "in close recess" within the lesser area. Milton has turned Euclidean space inside-out, as it were, in that infernal court.

To sum up, the mathematical structure of book 1 conveys the crossover from goodness to unalloyed evil as a passage from the infinite to the infinitesimal. The shrinkage of "Myriads of immortal Spirits" creates a dynamic metaphor of the fall from grace, but also suggests a mathematical parallel to the velocity of falling objects. And in fact, the action of book 1 gathers momentum at roughly the rate that Galileo ascribed to falling bodies—with a mighty acceleration at the end. In this way, Milton has drawn the "two new sciences" of the Enlightenment into his poem and marked for us the moment in history when the art of mathematics was becoming a precise instrument of physics, a period when conics and algebra, geometry and arithmetic, Cartesian space and number converged. We have traced the poet's strategic use of the zero and one as figural clusters, always paired, lending their shapes to heroic weapons, planetary bodies, geometric forms, gender symbols, and even to letters of the alphabet. One issue remains suspended: Why should Milton have chosen *zero* and *one* to represent the devil's party?

CARDINAL AMBIVALENCE

It has been demonstrated that Milton possessed a more than adequate knowledge of numerology and was acquainted with both the rabbinical and Pythagorean systems. Røstvig is surely on firm ground when she asserts his "first-hand acquaintance with the science of numbers both in its Platonic-Pythagorean form and in the Christianized version of the early Church Fathers."[39] In theological symbolism, the "circle" and "unity" are positive and signify constancy; like the triad of the Trinity, they refer to the Godhead. Fowler, as we have seen, recalls the hermetic doctrine of "God as simultaneous centre and circumference of the universal circle," while Milton himself, in *Christian Doctrine*, affirms that "God is ONE." It seems equally clear, however, that Milton includes the strict arithmetic sense of numbers in *Paradise Lost* as well as symbolic numerology, just as the poem entertains the older Ptolemaic system along with the newer Copernican physics.

In considering Milton's repeated use of *zero* and *one* to signify the action of the Fall, we need to distinguish the historical sense of the figures from their theological values. While both systems are in force in Milton's poem, they diverge in the most radical way: the meanings they yield stand in direct contradiction. Milton deliberately or intuitively chose these numbers for the following reasons: first, the contradictions that arise from the coexistence in the poem of contradictory philosophies of number are entirely germane to an entity who is undergoing a graduated change from angel to devil; second, the mathematical history of both these numbers reinforces the notion of inconstancy and ambivalence, independent of Christian doctrine; finally, the crucial topos of *mutability* in this Book—the fall into temporality, becoming, generation and corruption—determines Milton's choice of number. Let us see why.

Historically, the numbers *one* and *zero* have long been associated with inconstancy and contradiction. While modern mathematics does not trouble itself about the metaphysical unfitness of either to be called a number (covering them by special convention), both have been accounted disturbing anomalies—the monad as far back as Pythagoras.[40] In the chapter on *King Lear* we saw something of the contradictions locked into zero—Shakespeare's "O without a figure"—that date from its entrance into Western systems of accounting. Round zero suggests the divine perfection of the sphere, but also incessant change as an algorithmic "holding place." In itself, the cipher represents no numerical value. Milton, in fact, dangerously satirizes the newly restored king, Charles II, by charging that he sits at court "like a great cypher set to no purpose before a long row of other significant figures."[41] We found the same sequence, zero placed first, repeated in the original *figurae* of shield and spear with the "great cypher set to no purpose" on Satan's person. Paradoxically, *zero* symbolizes the All and signifies Nothing. The *one* is another such figure of contradiction.

The Pythagoreans held that the monad, although a source of numbers, was not itself a counting number. In Kramer's pragmatic terms, "there is no need to count in a set containing a unique, solitary pebble."[42] The number that Galileo, Descartes, and Pascal called "unity" does not itself manifest *plurality*—the attribute that for them, and for Milton, defines the category "Number." But while *one* denotes singularity, unity, the unmoving Parmenidean absolute, it also originates the digital system—for how can one begin to count without a countable individual? Hence its doubleness. Philosophically speaking, the *one* is able to signify changeless being and indicate temporal becoming. In like manner, Milton's Satan partakes of the unchanging yet continually changes. He is a deathless constant and at the same time the very principle of inconstancy.

The doubleness inherent in these two cardinal numbers has continued to occupy thinkers. In a contemporary study of mathematical concepts of infinity, José A. Benardete reflects on the questionable pair: "If zero remains anomalous even in formal mathematics, much the same is true of one. . . . You cannot divide any number into an equal part . . . so, too, you cannot *multiply* any number by one. You can only leave it alone. For us, as for the Greeks," he observes, "one is not a number [but] rather the beginning or source or principle which generates number." Following Wittgenstein, Benardete examines ordinary language as the matrix of number words. "Is *a* a number? Should the series of number-words read: none, a, two, three, etc.?" He concludes at this point that both zero and one are numbers "only in a derivative or tropological sense," which, he says, imparts to mathematical discourse "the interpretive flexibility of Scripture."[43] While zero and one have continued to elude concrete definition, and remain problematic in present-day logic and metaphysics, it is the mathematical climate of the late seventeenth century that most illuminates Milton's use of these figures in *Paradise Lost*. Paul de Man's commentary on Pascal's *Réflexions sur la géométrie en générale: De l'Esprit géométrique et l'Art de persuader* [44] helps to shed light on the subject.

Pascal's *Réflexions* dates from 1657 or 1658, just ten years before the appearance of *Paradise Lost*. In it, the French mathematician, logician, and mystic is engaged with some of the most advanced mathematical thought of his time: the notion of double infinity (the infinitely large and infinitely small); the nature of unity; and the problem of the *zéro/néant*. De Man, as one would expect, reads Pascal's *one* as an allegory of doubleness, while *zero* is placed outside the order of number entirely: "Whereas one is and is not a number at the same time, zero is radically not a number, absolutely heterogeneous to the order of number."[45] While one may justly question the psychological sources of de Man's critical preoccupation with doubleness and "undoing," his brilliant argument from the seventeenth-century *Réflexions* teaches us something directly about the coexistence of angelic intelligence and satanic duplicity within a single mind. With respect to Milton's text, the same argument shows precisely why the poet could rely upon zero and one to symbolize— almost to *perform*—the mystery of innate contradiction. To put it in a moral framework, it explains why these numbers could uniquely suggest the internal relations between good and evil.

Pascal's engagement with the infinitesimal calculus leads him to attempt a definition of zero and one, but it is the notion of infinite divisibility—the principle that fills Pandaemonium—that prompts "the truly Pascalian moment in the demonstration" according to de Man, i.e., the separation of number from geometry. Pascal begins by theorizing that "what applies to the individual unit of number, the *one*, does not apply to the indivisible unit of space," which leads him to consider the "real" and the merely "nominal" aspects of unity. On the one hand, it is "a mere name given to the entity that does not possess the properties of number"; on the other hand, the *one* "partakes" of number because it belongs to the same "species." And here Pascal comes up with his telling analogy of the house and the city: "[O]ne is of the same species as number, as a house is to a city, yet . . . one can always add a house to a city and it remains a city."[46] The *zero*, which Pascal has placed entirely outside number, nevertheless serves, in de Man's paraphrase, to join "the four intraworldly dimensions on which divine order exists"— that is, number, extension, duration, and motion—while it remains the essence of nothingness.

To return to Milton, this nascent sense of *zero* as the *néant* is conveyed through the celebrated image of the Godhead in the opening passage of *Paradise Lost:* the Spirit who "with mighty wings outspread / Dove-like satst brooding on the vast Abyss" (lines 20–21). The *néant*, at this point, is the "vast Abyss" made pregnant by the brooding Deity. It is of particular significance, then, that the poem's first mention of the Creator not only requires a trinity of words—"Thou O Spirit"—but that the vocative "O" forms their center. Here we see a *literal* representation of God as both "center" and "circumference" at the atomic level of the single letter-symbol. But the letter *O* is isomorphic with *zero*, just as the letter *I* shares the shape of the cardinal number *one*. The "O" in "Thou O Spirit" is able, therefore, to imply both the Divine Spirit and the theological *néant*, both the Creator and the potentiality out of which all created things emerge.

Clearly, both zero and one are peculiarly competent to express mathematical schizophrenia, at least so far as the seventeenth century perceived these figures. Both possess a double nature; both represent absolutes, on the one hand, and alteration, on the other—singularity and plurality, constancy and change. Both can suggest divine order but also daemonic unrest. Together they have an "interpretive flexibility" that accords perfectly with the poet's design. Milton is concerned, in book 1, with the loss of grace and the seizure of power on the grandest scale. He examines the realignment of virtue with vice within the corruptive framework of power politics. In a well-known fragment of the *Pensées*, Pascal twists might into right and strength into justice with seeming logic and great persuasiveness.[47] In much the same way, Milton's Arch-Rebel curves wrongdoing into right resistance with wicked logic, diabolical ambition into inspired exhortation: *All* is not lost!

The paired *figurae* that appear in different guises throughout book 1 support a binary logic of evil, forever welded to good. As mathematical entities, zero and one lend their tonic doubleness to the princely being turned power broker; the divided archangel remains a split figure of powerful negation and equally powerful presence. We see the same *figurae* reappear in book 2, when Satan stands poised on the verge of his own abyss, meditating mischief. Here at the edge of the "hoarie deep," the void, the space of limitless negation, Milton pictures the reverse face of Creation, and graphically sets forth the calculus of infinite loss:

> Illimitable Ocean without bound,
> Without dimension, where length, breadth, and highth,
> And time and place are lost. . . .

> (2.892–94)

4
Jamesian Geometry

Think of Henry James in the Piazza San Marco for the first time. Chances are he's sitting at Florian's Café absorbing "impressions," with something to drink before him, the great ducal palace across the square, and Ruskin's *Stones of Venice* in the pocket of his coat. "He came into Venice toward the end of a mid-September day," Leon Edel writes elegiacally, "when the shadows began to lengthen and the light to glow. He caught the distant sea-smell, glimpsed the water, the domes, the spires, and then the brown-skinned white-shirted gondolier swept him through the water amid slimy brick, battered marble, rags, dirt, decay." Decaying, gorgeous Venice fired James's imagination, and his biographer reports: "With Ruskin . . . in his pocket, he walked or floated through the city."[1] In the record of his first independent European travels, *Italian Hours*, the young James observes that Venice has had the "good fortune to become the object of passion to a man of splendid genius, who has made her his own," and adds, there is "no better reading at Venice therefore, than Ruskin."[2]

The author of *The Stones of Venice* was peculiarly alive to Euclidean forms and mathematical proportions in the city's architecture. Describing the facade of St. Michele of Lucca, he writes: "The morbid restlessness of the old designs is now appeased. Geometry seems to have acted as a febrifuge [medicine to reduce fever], for beautiful geometric designs are introduced amidst the tumult of the hunt."[3] One of Ruskin's meticulous sketches in *The Stones* shows the details of a "wall-veil decoration" set into the facade of a Venetian palace. Ranged around the sides of a diamond-shaped square, itself enclosing a circle or sphere, are a dove, a raven with dark wings outspread, a calf couchant, and a pair of lovebirds, all occupying the center of an elongated rectangle. Three large

XX.

Wall-Veil Decoration.

CA' TREVISAN.

J. Ruskin.

Ackermann, Lith. 319 Broadway N.Y.

"Wall-Veil" Decoration (Ca' Trevisan). Sketch by John Ruskin from *The Stones of Venice*. New York: John Wiley, 1851.

spheres placed horizontally command the geometric design. Ruskin describes the central emblems: "The dove, alighted, with the olive branch plucked off, is opposed to the raven with restless expanded wings. Beneath are evidently the two sacrifices 'of every clean fowl and of every clean beast.' The colour is given with green and white marbles, the dove relieved on a ground of greyish green, and all is exquisitely finished."[4]

One cannot know whether Ruskin's sketch or his description of the emblems on the Trevisan Palace made an impression on the young traveler, but clearly these same emblems might serve as a guide to the major characters in *The Wings of the Dove*, James's late, exquisitely finished novel. Similarly, the three parallel spheres of the wall-veil decoration recall the three great houses where its action is played out. In any case, James certainly integrated the larger geometries of Venice itself, including its famous square, into the work. "One has to read the pages consecrated to Venice in *The Wings of the Dove*," says James's biographer, "to discover how enduringly the spirit of the place entered into his life and art."[5]

James arrived in Venice in September 1869. Six months later, in March 1870, James's cousin, the spirited Minny Temple, died of tuberculosis at the age of twenty-four. When he learned of the death, James wrote to his mother: "Minny seemed such a breathing immortal reality that the mere statement of her death conveys little meaning."[6] She would never set foot in Italy, but her fictional avatar, Milly Theale, would spend her last months in Venice as a kind of sacred compensation. Some thirty years would intervene, however, between his beloved cousin's death and the appearance of Milly Theale. In the Trevisan wall-veil decoration, the raven's outspread wings suggest the powers of darkness and impending death. In James's novel, the dove too would finally spread her wings. James framed the last third of *Wings*—the scene of Milly's *agon*—in Venice; the beautiful dying city, as he wrote in the preface, was "the whole bright house of her exposure." I propose in this chapter to show that the elusive life of the novel is dependent to a large extent upon its geometry, its spatial structuring and design. The Venetian palace where Milly dies and achieves a "breathing immortality" is indeed the "bright house of her exposure," as James points out. But it is also the third house in the triptych of great houses that spatially order the action of the story—and that temporally order its progress.

Of the three late great novels, *The Wings of the Dove* (1902) is notable not only for delicately shaded portraiture and the tenuousness of its dialogue but for subtle swerves in the unfolding of its plot. On the part of the reader, it demands an ongoing reorientation toward each of its major characters, which contributes both to its difficulty and its beguilement. From the beginning it extended a monumental challenge. Ezra Pound called it "cobwebby," and Virginia Woolf wrote in her diary "one can never read it again."[7] R. P. Blackmur considered it James's flawed but transcendent masterpiece, while his earliest response to it demonstrates the immense fascination of the novel: having read it nonstop at seventeen, it apparently lured him into a lifetime of critical writing.

Although *Wings* has not accumulated the massive commentary that has gathered about *The Turn of the Screw*, it nevertheless remains an arena of cross-interpretation and critical debate. And, like the celebrated ghost story, it has generated questions of a fundamental nature with respect to its dramatis personae: Is the appealing, stricken Milly Theale its heroine, as James tells us in the preface, or is Kate Croy the "tragic protagonist," as F. W. Dupee has persuasively argued? Perhaps, as Quentin Anderson believes, the true hero is the young newspaperman, Merton Densher. Again, is Kate Croy her father's daughter gene-for-gene, the panther of the drawing-room jungle? or simply an underprivileged beauty with ravishing social presence and an extremely pragmatic "talent for life"? Is Milly's death tragic? redemptive? or existentially sardonic? What constitutes evil in the book's frame of morals? What kindles desire? Who is the villain?

In short, mystery and ambiguities proliferate in *Wings* from its so-called misplaced middle to the dramatic reversals of its codalike finale. Perhaps more than any other Jamesian work, *Wings* is burdened with the ghostly, impalpable weight of implication. The "cobwebby" indirectness of its discourse, the deliberate misdirection in its spoken dialogue, and the famous multiple embeddings of syntax are further compounded by James's heavy investment in sheer inference. Clearly one does not wish to reduce *Wings* to a tidy set of game rules, nor attempt to dispel all uncertainty—a quality as inherent in the life it mirrors as in the novel itself. Yet a serious consideration of the book's concrete structural symmetries—its internal geometry—will radically alter our perspective, modify our reading of character, and most importantly, illuminate the moral economy of the work. In other words, if we take James's account of his preliminary constructions at face value and apply what he tells us about the geometric design of his novels, then a dimension is revealed in *The Wings of the Dove* that sharpens our understanding of its fundamental conflict and of the complex relations of its characters. James, as we know, was preternaturally sensitive in the area of human relationships. "Universally, relations stop nowhere," he writes in *The Art of the Novel*, and the problem of the artist is "to draw, by a geometry of his own, the circle within which they shall happily appear to do so."[8]

To train the focus on the geometry of *Wings* is to reinforce its allegorical dimension and thereby to discover something of its ethical force. Such a perspective rather surprisingly places Lord Mark at the center of Milly's struggle with death and desire; it locates him, not merely as the vacant carrier of evil but as the material embodiment of wrongdoing in the work's moral economy. It suggests that Lord Mark, not Kate, is Milly's proper antagonist. Perhaps the best way to move toward this perspective is to allow James to define what he means by "a geometry of his own."

In the prefaces to the New York Edition, James describes himself not merely as a craftsman of language but as a draftsman who begins his work by plotting its geometry. This turns out to be more than a felicitous metaphor. In the preface to *The Awkward Age*, for example, James reconstructs for us his situational design, *actually drawn on paper* like an architect's rendering: "the neat figure of a circle consisting of a number of small rounds disposed at an equal distance about a central object. The central object," he explains, "was my situation, my subject in itself, to which the thing would owe its title, and the small rounds represented so many distinct lamps . . . the function of each of which would be to light with all due intensity one of its aspects" (*Art of the Novel*, 110). We learn further that certain "complications" make social occasions and human figures "difficult to isolate, to surround with the sharp black line, to frame in the square, the circle, the charming oval" (*Art of the Novel*, 101).

It is in the discussion of *Wings* that James most fully discloses his debt to Euclid, so feared and disparaged in his school days. Along with the familiar talk of "circles" and "centres," we are now introduced to solid cubes, squares, a spiral whirlpool, misplaced pivots, retreating points, relational lines and planes, and the engineering of pontics and piers in the formation of a fiction. No more than five or six years separates the actual publication of *Wings* and James's retrospective account of its production, which supports its credibility. Milly Theale, we are told in the preface, is the novel's subject and "centre," but the story will begin at the "circumference": "Though my regenerate young New Yorker . . . should form my centre, my circumference was every whit as treatable. . . . One began, in the event, with the outer ring, approaching the centre thus by narrowing circumvallations [the making of ramparts]"

(*Art of the Novel*, 294). Another passage in the preface concerns the process of drafting the original blueprint: "There was the 'fun,' to begin with of establishing one's successive centres—of fixing them so exactly that the portions of the subject commanded by them would constitute . . . *sufficiently solid blocks of wrought material, squared to the sharp edge, as to have weight and mass and carrying power*" (*Art of the Novel*, 296; my emphasis). Shortly thereafter, we learn that the London mansion called "Lancaster Gate" is part of a "constructional block" parallel to the Venetian palace. This is the first indication that the three great houses are more than mere backdrops. In terms of the novel's internal geometry, they acquire the solidity of foundation piers, firmly anchoring the action. James writes: "It is in Kate's consciousness that at the stage in question the drama is brought to a head, and the occasion on which, in the splendid saloon of poor Milly's hired palace, she takes the measure of her friend's festal evening, *squares itself to the same synthetic firmness as the compact constructional block inserted by the scene at Lancaster Gate*" (*Art of the Novel*, 301; my emphasis).

The occasion in the splendid saloon of poor Milly's hired palace is notable for a resonant geometric symbol—in the form of Milly's pearl necklace. Milly has chosen for her last festive appearance a "long, priceless chain, wound twice around her neck [which] hung heavy and pure, down the front of the wearer's breast."[10] Adeline Tintner, focusing on the portraiture in *Wings*, comments on the importance of the pearls: "Milly's 'royal ornament' becomes the 'symbol of differences' between herself and Kate. The exhibition of Milly's pearls," notes Tintner, "makes Densher see and understand what Kate wants him to do to make it possible for her to own such pearls." She believes the "center of the novel's composition is this scene that focuses on the pearls, in which Milly is made into a modern portrait by Sargent to balance the Bronzino and the Ravenna mural [a sixth century mosaic of Theodora]".[11] Tintner's reading leads one to perceive the ornament as a gesture of status. In support of such a reading, one recalls that in Venetian folklore a pearl of great price is cast by the doge into the sea. But I should like to suggest that the pearl chain hung around the girl's neck is a mathematical symbol describing her condition, as much as it serves to illustrate her wealth. The necklace forms a "charming oval," to use James's term, but it also frames the girl's figure in a *zero*. As a sign of Milly's condition it graphically, uncompromisingly, indicates how little time and life she has left.

Finally, we need to take up the "makeshift middle" or "misplaced pivot" of *Wings*, as James ruefully calls it. He means that he has given more space than he intended to the development of action that was primarily intended to provide background and contrast for Milly's predicament. We gather that the novel has rather gotten away from its author. But in the context of the novel's geometric design, the displacement is significant. As the result of an apparent miscalculation, *James has located the dramatic center of the work at its precise geometric center*, in book 5, at Matcham. In his own words, "The whole actual centre of the work, resting on a misplaced pivot and lodged in Book Fifth, pretends to a long reach . . . though bringing home to me, on reperusal, . . . the author's instinct everywhere for the *indirect* presentation of his main image" (*Art of the Novel*, 306). What is critical here is that James has pointed to one silent scene as the novel's "actual centre" and "main image": that charged tableau "deep within" Matcham, in which Lord Mark and Milly Theale stand facing the Bronzino portrait.

In short, to focus on the geometry of *Wings*—its "constructional blocks," circles, spheres, triangulations, the logic of its design carefully "squared to the sharp edge"—is to uncover an unexpectedly graphic dimension of emblem and allegory. To examine the actual center of the novel, the frozen moment of crisis in book 5, is to expose to view the play of good and evil that forms its spiritual axis. It is to reveal directly in visual terms, rather than by verbal indirection, the psychomachia at the heart of the work.[12] My object is not to reduce *Wings* to an Edwardian emblem book, but to demonstrate the relation of its spatial design to the development of its dramatic action. I want to make the case that James's fragile creation of atmosphere and ambiance, of tangential relationships and shifting balances of power, of hinted motives and cryptic dialogue—in short, the whole tragic, inexorable unfolding of plot, is made possible *only* because its weblike existence is anchored in geometric blocks that permit the novel's flights and transparencies by reason of their very concreteness.

Let us look briefly at what we get "up front," at the narrative *données* of the tale. We can then turn to the triptych of great houses, the Bronzino portrait, and the celebrated Venetian square that constitute the novel's structural *données*. What does happen in *The Wings of the Dove*? The story begins in London, moves to an English country estate, completes its primary scheme of action in Venice, and concludes with an epilogue that returns us, once more, to London. Kate Croy, a handsome, intelligent young woman with more ambition than means, fails to persuade her father to let her live with him. Lionel Croy is a swindler of immense charm and elegance, and this opening scene is crucial to the plot; it establishes a firm rationale for the attitudes and actions of the daughter, rejected outright in the one moment that we see her vulnerable. As Dupee notes, Kate's repeated cries of "Father!" only "provoke the most unpaternal cynicism from this brilliant portrait of total perversity. From this scene," he points out, "stems the desperation that undermines Kate's character."[13]

As a result of her father's refusal, she must submit her fortunes to the rich, childless, vulgar Aunt Maud—James's "Britannia of the Market Place"—who wishes to match her with a bald, middle-aged aristocrat. Lord Mark's ancestral holdings have dwindled to a country estate, but we understand that Aunt Maud is prepared to endow the couple handsomely if a marriage takes place. However, Kate and Merton Densher, a pleasant though indigent young journalist (apparently as "dense" as his name suggests), are engaged in a secret liaison. We see that Kate understands the proposed marriage as a vehicle, not to provide a "position" for herself alone, but through her aunt to provide for her father and her drab, complaining, widowed sister and brood (not since the Jellybys of *Bleak House* have we been party to such a revolting family scene).

Into this elaborate framework of family relations, social hierarchy, and market values steps James's heroine, Milly Theale. Young, naive, infinitely rich, and crowned with embarrassing flame-red hair, she is the single surviving heiress of old New York stock; and she is doomed, stricken with a mortal disease. "The case," James wrote, "prescribed for its central figure a sick young woman, at the whole course of whose consciousness one would have quite honestly to assist" (*Art of Novel*, 289). She travels with Susan Stringham, née Shepherd, a Boston widow who adores her and who was Aunt Maud's schoolmate.[14] Through her friend's connection with Maud Lowder, Milly becomes the rage of the London Season, and so reencounters the attractive Merton Densher, whom she had met briefly in New York.

The kindly specialist, Sir Luke Strett, confirms Milly's fears in one of the finest examples of Jamesian conveyance-by-indirection in the canon. He tells her, in effect, to go out and *live*, and suggests that love will be the best physic to ward off thoughts of death—or perhaps death itself. James himself tried to imbue Milly Theale with the "unsurpassable activity of passionate, of inspired resistance." "My young woman," he wrote, "would *herself* be the opposition—to the catastrophe announced by the associated Fates" (*Art of the Novel*, 289–90). Milly resolutely plans to "live."

The characters foregather at Matcham, Lord Mark's estate, a plutonian realm of whispering shades and "old gold." The owner takes Milly into the house to see his Bronzino, telling her that a striking resemblance obtains between the subject of the portrait and herself. As they stand looking at the picture—the central moment, I believe, of the novel—Milly absorbs the fact that the young woman in the painting is now "dead, dead, dead," and confronts her own approaching death at the same time. The symbolism is heavily laid on at this point; the stream of Milly's thoughts tells us that she is grasping the knowledge that her future is a thing of the past, that she is, in a way, staring at her own dead self. Sharon Cameron glosses her thoughts with sensitivity: "Milly, looking at the portrait, rather thinks of the woman out of the portrait, not existing in a frame, but existing in time," and thus "projects the image of the lady forward from the moment of the painting and projects the image of herself backward; in the intersection of those moments resemblance is located: she sees the woman as she sees herself, another woman who is dying."[15]

Like a calculating chess player, Lord Mark now makes his move; he lets Milly know he would like to "take care of her." However, unaware of the understanding between Kate and Densher, Milly has fallen in love with the young man and she has no interest in Lord Mark's offer. James's own comment on the peer's proposal is illuminating. In his working notebook on *Wings* we find James construing "such a remedy" as "sufficiently second-rate":

It has bothered me in thinking of the little picture—this idea of the physical possession, the brief physical, passional rapture which at first appeared essential to it; bothered me on account of the ugliness, the incongruity, the nastiness, *en somme*, of the man's "having" a sick girl: also on account of something rather pitifully obvious and vulgar in the presentation of such a remedy for her despair—and such a remedy only. "Oh, she's dying without having had it? Give it to her and let her die"—that strikes me as sufficiently second-rate.[16]

In Venice, Milly rents the Palazzo Leporelli with the assistance of the doting Susan and an Italian entrepreneur named Eugenio who, as James tells us through Milly, has measured the exact capacity of her pocket. Here Kate broaches her Machiavellian plan to her lover: Densher is to accept Milly's affection and marry the American girl; when she dies, he will be very, very rich, and he and Kate can then marry. Densher is caught in Hamlet-like ambivalence and with the same paralyzing effect. But James moves swiftly now to resolve the whole cluster of subplots, pulling in his tricks in quick succession: we are given sex in Venice, violence in Venice, and finally death in Venice. Densher pressures Kate to a sexual surrender; Lord Mark revenges himself brutally for Milly's rejection by informing Milly of their engagement. Bereft of hope, Milly turns her face to the wall and dies.

The novel does not end here, just as in James's metaphysics "relationships stop nowhere." Its ending is the work's chief irony and quite possibly its chief beauty. In the epilogue we discover that Milly has left her entire fortune to Densher after all. He hands it over to Kate, but forces her to choose between the legacy and himself—he will not marry her if she accepts it. Kate chooses the money, realizing one-third of the gamble: her original stake was for the money, Merton, and marriage—all three. Her resolute "We shall never be again as we were!" sums up the pragmatics of the tale, but also Densher's evolution, or conversion, or altered understanding of what is good and what is not good. We understand, by means of this change, that when Milly is at the end of her long dying, when she is isolated, betrayed, and deprived of the experience she craves, by some spiritual convulsion she has been able to transmute her passion into a transcendent lovemaking of no small potency. So James draws his circle fully round, for as he says in the preface to *Wings*, "[W]hat a tangled web we weave when . . . mislaying or otherwise trifling with our blest pair of compasses" (*Art of the Novel*, 302).

MATCHAM, MILLY, MARK

The novel's internal geometry is formed largely on the square and the triangle. It has four major characters who for various reasons are entertaining the idea of marriage, and this quartet like any other square contains implicit triangles. Its denouement occurs in St. Mark's Square, "the splendid Square which bears the patron's name and which is the centre of Venetian life," as James noted in *Italian Hours*. Lord Mark, who shares the patron's name, is worth noting in the context of a structuring geometry. He is the character who seems a perfect nonentity, who most lacks human dimension, and whose very name ironically suggests the Euclidean definition of a *point*—"That which lacks all dimension and has position only."

In the foreground is the triptych of great houses: Lancaster Gate, Matcham, and the Palazzo Leporelli.[17] Taken together, they depict a history of degenerating social position and, if one moves back in time, of increasing remoteness between social castes. Lancaster Gate is the house of the present, built and inhabited by a powerful merchant class; Matcham is the house of the not too distant past, of landed gentry, the feudal lords of an agricultural economy; Palazzo Leporelli is the house of the distant past, built as a fortress of sorts for a powerful aristocracy. In 1887, as Percy Lubbock tells us, James made two long visits to Venice, the second time staying with friends in "the splendid old palazzo Barbaro, where years afterwards he placed the exquisite and stricken heroine of *The Wings of the Dove*."[18] The Venetian palace completes the history told by the book's great houses. Like Matcham, it represents a dead nobility, faded glory, and present corruption. It stands like a beautiful empty seashell within which parasites make their abode.

Matcham is the archetypal site of exchange in *Wings*. It forms the center panel that links the trio of great houses, but its symmetry extends also to its name—which not only suggests "matchmaking" but is appropriately palindromic. Temporally, Matcham looks to the past and future at once: it represents a lost way of life, a shrinking social realm; the Venetian painting, its central icon, predicts for Milly the death that is to come *and* the place it will occur. Thus the Bronzino situated "deep within" Matcham—i.e., set at the precise center of the triptych's central panel—establishes more than any other iconic emblem in the novel an equation of past-future symmetry. It projects a demonic "universe of death," a fatalistic philosophy of irrevocable repetition—exactly the tonal ambiance that must be heard and felt in Lord Mark's lair.

In his record of travels in Italy James mentions no portrait of a lady by Bronzino, but his description of a "smallish canvas of Sebastian del Piombo," a painting he found in the Church of San Giovanni Crisostomo, in Venice, seems to have made a deep impression on him—and it serves as a gloss for the portrait at Matcham. "This face and figure are almost unique among the beautiful things of Venice," James writes, "and they leave the susceptible observer with the impression of having made, or rather having missed, a strange, a dangerous, but a most valuable acquaintance." The lady in the portrait, we are told, is "superbly handsome" and "the typical Venetian of the sixteenth century." Here the young James waxes eloquent, couching his appreciation in Paterian cadences: "Never was there a greater air of breeding, a deeper expression of tranquil superiority. She walks a goddess. . . . It is impossible to conceive a more perfect expression of the aristocratic spirit either in its pride or in its benignity." But for all this, concludes the discerning young observer, "there are depths of possible disorder in her light-colored eye" (*Italian Hours*, 31-32). We can see something of Milly here in James's "magnificent creature," something of Kate, and surely something of the portrait at Matcham.

The portrait of the Venetian lady is part of the tableau that defines the moral conflict of the work, for Milly is not only "mirrored" in the Bronzino, she is here confronted with Lord Mark. Indeed, this is the crux of it. In the tableau of man, woman, and painting, we are shown not one but two "Marks." Milly, of course, is Lord Mark's marriage target, his very particular "mark." Antipathetic, innately antagonistic, the positive and the negative "Marks" are as evenly matched as two queens on a chessboard. At Matcham, we are meant to see the game in its crudest form, from the point of view of its owner, and in both senses of the word—game as *play* and game as *prey*. In visual proximity and in fact, we are shown Lord Mark and his *objective*, the pursuer and the pursued, the hunter and his "game." The Bronzino forms the third element in the composition of this scene, and the painting—the hanging lady—exists as the point on which the antagonists fix their regard, and a place where both perspectives meet. In a manner of speaking, both Milly and Mark "vanish" into the painting, the one into its aesthetic past and the other into its premonition of a lethal future.

James has intuitively set the scene of the psychomachia at the exact middle of the novel. The antagonists are both battling for their very lives. Mark can recover past ease, comfort, and station only by means of a vampire victory—he needs to suck Milly dry in order to exist as he has been existing. In this sense, he represents the ontology of repetition, inexorable repetition of what has been. Milly, on the other hand, must battle her physical disease and her despair, with this sophisticated antagonist on her flank. And yet, to turn the meaning around once more, she is as "game" as they come. With passionate, inspired resistance, she will yield neither to her own despair nor to others' greed, and James has subtly hinted this in the dialogue that ends the tableau.

At the moment in which the girl grasps her own imminent death, James introduces a seeming paradox. Looking at the portrait through tears, Milly reflects that its subject "was dead, dead, dead." But then James tells us: *"Milly recognised her exactly in words that had nothing to do with her. 'I shall never be better than this.'"* Only in retrospect are we able to see in this phrase the sense of "I shall never be *more good*," and hence the moment that prepares the gift to Densher that can never be acknowledged. That the words "had nothing to do with" the dead Venetian or the dead past strongly suggests that "I shall never be better" is more than a reference to failing health. It is a premonition of her victory over the domain of Lord Mark, and it arrives at the exact moment she recognizes her mortality. "Book Fifth is a new block mainly in its provision of a new set of occasions," says James in the preface, "I have by this time all the choice of those who are to brush the surface with a dark wing" (*Art of the Novel*, 305).

In a paper entitled "Evolutionary Love" Charles Saunders Peirce, engaging the theology of Henry James Sr., startlingly defines evil as "one of the major perfections of the Universe."[19] James Sr. and the logician are manifestly attacking the doctrine of God's perfect self-love. Peirce asserts that "self-love is no love," hence "if God's *self* is love, that which he loves must be a *defect* of love; just as a luminary can light up only that which must otherwise be dark."[20] James Sr. similarly distinguishes between "creaturely love" (love of that which conforms with one's self) and "creative Love, all whose tenderness . . . must be reserved only for what intrinsically is most bitterly hostile and negative to itself." Peirce, however, having determined that the logical conclusion of the elder James's theory posits God as the primary lover of evil, ends his review on a wonderfully ironical note: "Obviously no genius could make his every sentence as sublime as one which discloses for the problem of evil its everlasting solution." Peirce's familiarity with the Swedenborgian's theory, his examining attitude, and especially the delicate irony might as easily have been expressed by the elder James's son and namesake. But like his father, and certainly like his brother, William, the younger Henry James engaged energetically with the problem of malevolence in people's lives.

Evil, as such, attains a rare visibility in *Wings of the Dove*. Unlike its ghostly manifestation in *The Turn of the Screw*, or in "The Jolly Corner," the demonic is incarnated in a living character in *Wings*. When it can draw power from silence, it remains silent; when it can do mischief by speaking, it speaks. Significantly, James has invested the active principle of evil in a largely passive antagonist. Lord Mark is singularly "insubstantial," as Dupee has pointed out, but James has disguised him to resemble the other members of the cast. As a character who lacks dimension, who seems bland and innocuous, he has remained largely unremarked. Yet it seems appropriate, in this novel, that the character who embodies malevolence verges on the invisible until the final killing utterance. James reinforces his virtual absence as a "personality" by a rhetorical strategy: the "dialogue" assigned to Lord Mark is, to a remarkable extent, a repetition of the syllable "Oh!" In fact, as Sallie Sears has noted, Milly assesses him as a man who is "familiar with everything, but conscious of *nothing*," who has "*no* imagination" (*Wings*, chap. 19, p. 162); and a man who "pointed to *nothing*; which was very possibly just a sign of his real cleverness, one of those that the really clever had in common with the really *void*" (178). Lord Mark may be devoid of personality, but he exists more as a representation of the void rather than as a fully realized character. In a way, he personifies what the James family called a "vastation," the father's term for his own terrifying experience of the abyss.[21]

In *The Negative Imagination*, Sallie Sears perceives "something of a hellish chess game in the book's presentation of the mathematics of narrowing alternatives."[22] The order that operates in James's novels is "a negative, a diabolic one, a geometry of destruction, an order . . . of powers conspiring to a sinister end and, with their command of means, finally achieving it."[23] Sears places Lord Mark at the innocuous end of her spectrum of negation. It seems to me, however, that it is precisely this quality of the void, his lethal blandness, his nonchalance, the nothingness of his "Oh's," the vacancy of his presence, the meaningless whisperings in his house, that sharply differentiates Lord Mark from the fleshed-out characters of the novel and casts him as the power of extreme negation.

His name has been well and deliberately chosen for its connotations of murder, money, and the market—no less than for its connections with the Ducal Palace and Piazza San Marco. I have already touched on the sense of "mark" as the one to be taken advantage of, or hunted down. Another gloss of the term defines "mark" as invisible currency. Unlike the deutsche mark, which is still a "working" currency, the English mark was a "money of account," that is, a specific amount of silver placed on an exchequer board for land taxes but *never actually coined*. As a lord who labors not, as a parasite who contributes nothing, whose station yet accords him an "invisible currency," Lord Mark embodies the negative power in *Wings*. He is like a vortex, sucking all toward itself, into an abyss of greed. His pernicious, corrupt nature, his vengeful *crudeltà*, and his banality are all brought together in the scene where Densher discovers him seated in the square that bears his name. Here, in St. Mark's Square—"the drawing-room of Europe," as James put it—he sits as the emblematic Lord of Exchange.

The denouement in James's "splendid Square . . . which is the centre of Venetian life" contributes to the novel's dramatic inexorability. But in what sense does its *location* inform the scene? It is important, in this context, to recall that from James's point of view (and Ruskin's), the Ducal Palace and the Piazza represented singular beauty—but also disease, death, incurable decay, and a degraded commerce. "The misery of Venice stands there for all the world to see" James writes in *Ital-*

ian Hours. "The Venetian people have little to call their own. . . . Their habitations are decayed; their taxes heavy; their pockets light; their opportunities few" (*Italian Hours,* 5). Venice, he feels, is "the most melancholy of cities [and] the most beautiful of tombs," yet its decay is undeniably aesthetic: "Decay is in this extraordinary place golden in tint and misery *couleur de rose*" (*Italian Hours,* 65).

James's strongest reservation at the time of his first visit had to do with the commercial debasement of "the City of St. Mark," and this is particularly meaningful when we consider Densher's encounter with Lord Mark in that same square. For the young James, the sanctuary was a locus of dishonor "infested" by tour guides, pimps, and peddlers: "The condition of this sanctuary is surely a great scandal," he writes. "The pedlars . . . ply their trade—often a very unclean one—at the very door of the temple; they follow you across the threshold, into the sacred dusk, and pull your sleeve, and hiss in your ear, scuffling with each other for customers." He concludes: "There is a great deal of dishonour about St. Mark's altogether, and if Venice . . . has become a great bazaar, this exquisite edifice is now the biggest booth." But there is another significant quality to be experienced at this site: "Still, it is almost a spiritual function—or, at the worst, an amorous one—to feed one's eyes on the molten colour that drops from the hollow vaults" (*Italian Hours,* 13–14)

Here in the "great bazaar," directly across the square from the Ducal Palace, James has the young newspaperman spot Lord Mark through the plateglass window of Florian's Café—reading a newspaper. The "news" is Densher's moment of truth. At this point he grasps not only what *Mark* has done—or undone—but what he himself has been party to. Dupee suggests that the parasitic Eugenio, Densher, and Lord Mark appear in this chapter as three aspects of the overarching greed that bedevils Milly throughout and finally helps to kill her. Clearly, to see Lord Mark through a reflecting pane of glass in the debauched and commercialized, yet amorously beautiful, locus of St. Mark's Square is to see Densher squarely confronting his own corrupted self. The shock of identification with the other "con artist" is the recognition that immediately and positively changes him. This is the moment that logically underwrites the ascetic self-denial and the *caritas* that permeates his final scene with Kate, for he can now align himself with the spiritual force and generosity of the dead girl. The great four-sided square is thus made the site of Densher's moral upheaval, just as the framed Bronzino exists as Milly's "vanishing point," so to speak, and the site of her imminent transcendence.

From this perspective, it appears that the geometry of *The Wings of the Dove* functions as a silent guide to the novel's psychological drama. The historian H. V. Routh asserted with some justice that Henry James, far from creating characters who "live in a calm, sad, very polite twilight of the volition," was in fact a pragmatist who had "invented fascinating and ingenious hypotheses; problems of upper-class ethics and psychology, which he then [sat] down to solve as if he were illustrating an idea extracted from one of his brother William's treatises." James's ability to reveal the unexpected aspects of Victorian gentility, said Routh, made his "complex and labyrinthine" novels into guidebooks, as it were, to the art of "transforming experience into moral speculation."[24] In this context, it seems entirely possible that the Trevisan Palace wall design supplies a geometric framework for the moral design of James's novel, and further, that John Ruskin's description of its emblems sheds light on the novel's resolution. [25]

One can generalize the central drama in *Wings* as a struggle between the principle of corruption "brushing the surface with a dark wing" and the Jamesian principle of *conversion*, having for its icon "the dove alighted, with the olive branch plucked off." As R. W. B. Lewis observes, the tale "succeeds almost uncannily in begetting a mystic consciousness and a religious experience out of the unredeemably human and earthbound modern Anglo-American world."[26] In *Wings*, too, geometry has acted as a kind of febrifuge. What we find at the last is that Milly—the novel's primary "object of passion"—has transmuted cold yellow metal into spiritual force, exchanged betrayal for generosity, deception for compassion. Her clean sacrifice has neutralized demonic energy, greed, and hauteur, and the overwhelming vacancy of evil has been filled with something good. Yet, all is not well.

Milly, like her whole family line, is dead. The three great houses remain as the foundation piers of the tale, suggesting that the progression from greed to corruption to final dissolution will repeat itself in an ongoing cycle. The Venetian portrait that James makes so central to the architecture of *Wings* invites us to scan back in time to a young woman's death and forward to another young woman's death. The portrait thus functions as a kind of temporal triptych—an icon of past and future mortality conjoined with the tableau of the present moment—set deep inside a house of shades.

Some thirty-five years after the publication of *Wings*, Jorge Luis Borges defined yet another Jamesian portrait as a "nexus between past and present."[27] Tracing the motif of a temporal paradox from Coleridge to H. G. Wells to "the sad and labyrinthine Henry James," Borges analyzes James's *The Sense of the Past* as a variation or elaboration of Wells's *Time Machine:* "James's protagonist returns . . . to the eighteenth century, by identifying himself with that period," observes Borges, and—like the Bronzino portrait in *Wings*—James's vehicle to the past is "a picture . . . that mysteriously represents the protagonist. Fascinated by this canvas, he succeeds in going back to the day it was painted [and meets] the artist, who paints him with fear and aversion" because he senses something uncanny in "those future features." This portrait, too, functions as a temporal nexus where past and future meet.

Characteristically, Borges's focus of interest in James's unfinished novel is the notion of infinite regression he finds at its center: "James thus creates an incomparable *regressus in infinitum* when his hero . . . returns to the eighteenth century because he is fascinated by an old painting, but [the hero's] return to this century is a condition for the existence of the painting."[28] Hence the built-in paradox that so intrigues the Argentine: "The cause follows the effect, the reason for the journey is one of the consequences of the journey."[29] In this framework of cool logic, Borges, the student of mazes and ghostly recurrences, ponders the uncompleted project of the master.

5

Borges:
"Algebra and Fire"

Borges recalls in a memoir that his father—"a philosophical anarchist"—
conferred two great gifts upon him. He "revealed the power of poetry
to me—the fact that words are not only a means of communication but
also magic symbols and music." His father also gave the child his first
lessons in formal logic, making of it a kind of game: "When I was still
young, he showed me, with the help of a chessboard, the paradoxes of
Zeno—Achilles and the tortoise, the unmoving flight of the arrow, the
impossibility of motion."[1]

Written over a span of some fifty years, Borges's jewel-like essays
and parables, even his poems, attest to an ongoing preoccupation with
number, algebra, and geometry. André Maurois drew attention to his
"tight, almost mathematical style" in a preface to *Labyrinths* (1964). His
detective stories quite pointedly contain a mathematical dimension, as
John Irwin has shown in his superb analysis of Borges as a literary dop-
pelgänger of Poe.[2] Apart from direct references to a score of celebrated
mathematicians and their concepts, Borges is repeatedly engaged with
subjects that partake of a mathematical nature: games, chance, chess,
probability, set theory, uncertainty, infinity, random and repeating series, identity, and doubling. Not least, one senses the bewitchment for
Borges of the kind of unresolvable paradox that, like some tripodal
monster, has a leg in philosophy, in mathematical logic, and in fiction.

I would argue that it is precisely this mind-set—his deliberate engagement with number *as such* in the realm of story, the deployment of
Euclidean forms as a dramatic component of plot—that imparts to
Borges's writing its unique character. It is his bent for the mathematical, as Maurois discerned, that lends his style its lapidary precision,
its lexical spareness, its distilled formulations, its Spinozan ethic, its

playful Carrollian flights, its elegance—in short, its signature. But this same predisposition fosters the labyrinthine complexities of Borges's *ficciones*, the mirrorlike repetitions and returns, the "nested" elements, the intimations of infinite regress, and, above all, the enigmas, the riddles, the unsolved problems. And surely this same turn of mind encourages his flirtation with outrageous abstractions.

"The Aleph" is a particularly good example of Borges's ability to integrate mathematical concepts into his stories without allowing the mathematics to overwhelm the narrative. This is not a case of characters talking *about* a mathematical conundrum as part of the dialogue, in a trivial or nontrivial way, but something more fundamental to fiction. In "The Aleph," Borges is using algebra, transfinite number, and geometry to shape the action and to develop the psychology of his characters. In addition, at the simplest "atomic" level, Borges's tale about an *aleph* shows how a single letter, number, or geometric figure may be made to resonate complex information—like his father's "magic symbols."

I propose, therefore, to move to a reading of this romantic and enigmatic tale by way of its mathematical constructs. I want to establish Borges's familiarity with such constructs, and to distinguish his forays into mystical numerology (the literature of the Cabala, the multiple cosmologies of the Gnostics) from his discussions of pure mathematics and mathematical logic. While these represent opposed models in the universe of number, Borges is clearly interested in its symbolic as well as its rational aspects.

ALPHANUMEROLOGY

Before turning to the more orthodox mathematics in his essays and fiction, it will be helpful to explore what lies beneath Borges's intrigue with the alphanumerical mysteries of the Cabala.[3] Most studies of his use of number have concentrated on this "mystical" aspect, and Borges himself maintained a continuing interest in the medieval doctrines of the Gnostics and Cabalists, and the practice known as *gematria*, a method of interpretation of the Hebrew scriptures based upon the numerical value of the letters in the words.[4] However, it should be emphasized that while this cultivated, ironic Argentine seems drawn to the occult computations of *Zohar* and the Cabala, he does not necessarily "believe in" the mythic conjectures of eleventh-century rabbis, nor swallow whole the Gnostic doctrine of emanations so closely connected with the Cabala, and earlier with Plotinus.[5] James Irby points out that throughout Borges's writings, "his cosmologies are like hypotheses, cherished but also problematical, as the whole tentative, self-critical style . . . indicates."[6] Borges, who is something of a philosophical multiculturalist, is interested in the problem of evil; the concept of infinity exerts a similar pull. His beloved *Britannica* tells him that the medieval doctrines in question were formulated, at least in part, to account for the existence of evil in this world, and to link a finite universe to an infinite Godhead. Perhaps, for Borges, there is some understanding to be gained from the alphanumerical manipulations of the rabbis.

But there is another aspect to consider. One approach to Borges's preoccupation with magical symbols—which is manifest in tales like "The God's Script"—is to trace the origin of written number back to early alphabet systems. This is not as tangential as it may seem. Cabalistic hermeneutics depends absolutely upon the cohesion of letter and number, and this kind of interpretive interchange goes back to a stage of development when *a numeral does not possess its own representative symbol, but exists as an alternative rendering of the letter symbol*. (The principle does not obtain in all languages, but in Hebrew and Greek, for instance, the identity of letter and number holds true). The encyclopedist of the *Britannica* states that the numerical value of letters was obvious and striking when no ciphers existed: "[A] combination of consonants would automatically suggest either a word or a total, and the connection between the two would not seem . . . farfetched."[7]

In the beginning, as is well known, the Hebrew letters *aleph* and *beth* also meant "one" and "two." The twenty-four books of the *Iliad* are "numbered" from book *Alpha* to book *Omega*, using all twenty-four letters of the Greek alphabet, and suggesting the same global completeness indicated by the phrase "from A to Z." The very notions of cardinality (one, two, three) and ordinality (first, second, third) are implicit in the ready-made *sequence* of the letters in an alphabet or syllabary. What we perceive, then, is the origin of a number system in an already established system of letter symbols. There exists a literal "scripture" or writing that primarily signifies phonetic values, but which also displays the necessary discreteness and continuity required for enumeration. In his lecture on the Cabala, we find Borges remarking on the *priority of the written letter*, the Cabalists' belief that the letter-symbol, not the word, is the first instrument of God.

A final note. During the late eleventh century, a curious reversal (anticipated by Diophantes in the third century) began to take place: letter symbols were introduced into the number system. Carl Boyer's history of mathematics records a transitional period in both the Greek and Hebrew number systems, just before the implementation of Hindu-Arabic numerals and positional notation: "In the Byzantine culture the first nine Greek alphabetic numerals, supplemented by a special zero symbol, took the place of the Hindu numerals." At the same time, Boyer adds, Abraham Ibn Ezra (ca. 1090–1167) introduced a similar scheme, using "the first nine Hebraic alphabetic numerals, and a circle for zero."[8] The Hindu-Arabic *zero* had been introduced into European methods of accounting by the Italian Fibonacci and the mysterious (German?) monastic, Jordanus Nemorarius (who seems like a character invented by Umberto Eco, or Borges himself). In Boyer's account, the thirteenth-century *Arithmetica* of this same Nemorarius is "significant especially for the use of letters instead of numerals as numbers, thus making possible the statement of general algebraic theorems."[9] The development of algebra in western mathematics completes the reversal: quantities come to be represented by letter symbols, as the familiar a, b and x, y and Σ, the Greek sigma.

It is this root interchangeability of number and word, its *transformational* aspect, suggestive of endless interpretive possibilities, that so charms Borges—a charm enhanced, doubtless, by the double-faced nature of the letter symbol, its history of inherent Siamese-twinship with number. The letter/number may be said to enjoy a "monstrous" partnership, to use Borges's adjective of inexplicability, which brings us to his writings on the Cabala.

A glance at an early essay and a lecture published some forty-five years later should establish Borges's view with respect to mystical numerology. "A Vindication of the Cabala" (1931) evenhandedly attacks both the Cabala and Catholic doctrine, and appears to set forth Borges's position toward mystical doctrine unequivocally. Approximately one-half of the "Vindication" is spent on the "monstrous" notion of the Trinity. This doctrine of "three inexplicable persons," says Borges, conveys "intellectual horror, a strangled, specious infinity like that of opposite mirrors."[10] Borges treats the triple Godhead of Catholicism as he will later treat the golem of the rabbis in the *Zohar*. They are both "intonations" of a recurring metaphor—in this case, the magical creation that grows uncontrollably beyond all bounds.

Far from devising an apologia for cabalistic doctrine, which the title leads one to expect, Borges states at the outset that he is concerned primarily with its hermeneutical or cryptographic procedures. These are swiftly cataloged: "the vertical reading of sacred texts, the reading referred to as *boustrophedon* (one line from left to right, the following line from right to left), the methodical substitution of certain letters of the alphabet for others, the sum of the numerical value of the letters." Borges is enumerating the algorithms of the Cabala; his interest lies in the specific technical operations by which interpretations of the text may be generated.

At the close of the "Vindication," Borges uses two separate frames to discuss the Cabalists' approach to Scripture, the first mathematical and the second metaphorical. The premise that God has "dictated" the contents of the Holy Books word-for-word, he says, "makes of the Scriptures an absolute text, where the collaboration of chance can be calculated at zero." The second reference moves from the language of mathematical probability to that of revelation. The Scriptures undergo a transformation from "book" to "light" by way of an ascending parataxis: "A book impenetrable by contingency, a mechanism of infinite purpose, of infallible variations, of revelations lying in wait, of superimposed light." The flight of rhetoric is cut short by a talmudic ending—a question about the text that answers itself, and at the same time has no answer: "How could one not question it to absurdity, to numerical excess, as did the Cabala?" What has been vindicated is neither the Cabala nor its doctrines, but Borges's evident fascination with the poetics of "numerical excess."

While the Cabala remains for him a paradigm of exegetical excess, the later Borges seems more interested in the Gnostic and cabalistic approach to the "essential problem, the existence of evil." Why did Jehovah create this world "so full of errors, so full of horror, so full of sins, so full of physical pain, so full of guilt, so full of crime?" Borges suggests that the Cabalists and Gnostics resolved it by declaring that the universe was the work of a deficient Divinity, so far down in the series of emanations that his "fraction of Divinity approaches zero."[11] In the later essay, Borges emphasizes the priority of the letters of the sacred text. Cabala "believes that the letters came first, that they were the instruments of God, not the words signified by the letters," and he remarks, almost in Derrida's words, "It is as if one were to think of writing, contrary to experience, as older than the speaking of the language."[12] As in the earlier essay, the absence of chance is heavily underscored: "Nothing . . . can be accidental in the Scriptures; everything must be predetermined, including, for example, the number of letters in each verse." Borges distances himself from the Cabala, at the end, by aligning himself with George Bernard Shaw and the rationalist theory that man is in the process of creating God: "If we are magnanimous" says Borges, "if we are intelligent, if we are lucid, we will be helping to construct God."

What, exactly, draws Borges to these medieval doctrines? We find certain elements recurring in his discussions of them: (1) their systematic framework, (2) the construct of an absolutely determined cosmos, (3) the near-obsessional manipulation of letters and numbers, (4) the notion that letters came first, (5) the concern with human—and divine— imperfection, and (6) the identification of the divinity as an author, "emanating" a diminishing series of lesser creative beings. Finally, as noted earlier, Borges is familiar with the specific algorithms or techniques that numerology invented for diagnostic purposes, and quite probably he is intrigued by the esoteric relationship the Cabalists presume between malleable word and intractable number.

His discussions of "pure" mathematics call up quite another constellation. Borges was thoroughly capable of expounding the concepts treated in Kasner and Newman's *Mathematics and the Imagination,* a book he reviewed for *Sur* in 1940, as Irwin has noted.[13] Algebra, geometry, set theory, and mathematical descriptions of infinity are intrinsic to his thinking and stimulate his imagination. His writings return to certain mathematical ideas repeatedly. We can turn now to Borges on "volumes" of sand, irrational numbers, infinite regress, quadratic equations, and transfinite sets.

ARCHIMEDES, OMAR, CANTOR

Karl Menninger's encyclopedic history of number states that Archimedes' *Sand-reckoner* "proposed to count the seemingly uncountable by creating a number sequence . . . which could count all the grains of sand contained in a sphere the size of the universe."[14] Menninger points to Archimedes' "infinitesimal analysis" as the major achievement of this "most original and creative of all the Greek mathematicians" and notes some of the advances in geometry it made possible: "new insights into the measurement of the circle, the volumes of bodies bounded by curved surfaces, the areas of plane figures with curvilinear edges." Archimedes' treatise dates back to the third century B.C., and Menninger carefully outlines its mathematical/verbal project: Archimedes wished "to show by counting the sands that the ordinary Greek number sequence, which went only as far as *myrioi,* could in principle be extended without limit, and that any imaginable number could thereby be expressed verbally." In other words, the *Sand-reckoner's* project was to *name a number* that encompasses everything countable.[15]

Borges's semiautobiographical fable, "The Book of Sand," was first published in 1975 as "El libro de arena." Taken together with "The Total Library" (1939), "The Library of Babel" (1941), and with Tzinacán's dream of the endless grains of sand in "The God's Script," the story suggests more than a nodding acquaintance with Archimedes' *Sand-reckoner*.[16] Written in the late period, "The Book of Sand" also demonstrates its author's ongoing preoccupation both with geometry and "irrational" number series—that is, numbers (such as pi) that cannot be expressed as whole numbers or fractions but only as an infinitely long decimal, continuing randomly, with no sequence repeating.[17] In the Borges lexicon, such "monstrous" numbers translate into linear labyrinths.

The tale, narrated in the first person, concerns the purchase of an infinite book—a Volume of all Volumes—by a retired librarian who eventually disposes of what he perceives to be a diabolical artifact by "losing" it in the subterranean reaches of his own library. The tale's opening sentence suggests both infinite geometric expansions and endless interspersions:

> The line is made up of an infinite number of points; the plane of an infinite number of lines; the volume of an infinite number of planes; the hypervolume of an infinite number of volumes. . . . .[18]

The key term, *volume*, joins geometry to written words and spoken language. While the opening meditation traces the history of geometry from dimensionless Euclidean points to contemporary multidimensional systems, Borges cuts off the train of thought with "volumes"— the plural grammatical "number." In Spanish, English, and German, "volume" denotes *spatial quantity*; it denotes a *bound book*; it refers to *intensity of sound*. In "The Book of Sand," Borges uses "volume" to signify a written text—the Book itself—and "hypervolume" to suggest an extraordinary enlargement, the sense of an "overtext" or "super book." But "hypervolume," which Borges borrows from multidimensional geometry, is also meant to indicate a mathematical monstrosity: the pages of the uncanny book follow no discernible order. They are numbered as unsystematically as the series of pi. In the narrator's words: "I opened the book at random. The script was strange to me. The pages . . . were laid out in double columns, as in a Bible. . . . In the upper corners of the pages were Arabic numbers. I noticed that one left-hand page bore the number (let us say) 40,514 and the facing right-hand page 999. I turned the leaf: it was numbered with eight digits" ("Book of Sand," 118). Unlike the absolute text of the "Vindication," this tome is ruled by a principle of chance.

The Archimedean project of finding a number to represent a whole universe of sand is brought to a successful conclusion in Kurd Lasswitz's "The Universal Library,"[19] cited by Borges in his own mathematical fantasy, "The Total Library" (*Borges, A Reader*, 94–96). Lasswitz's "story" (a mathematical problem set forth verbally) was first published in the original German when Borges was two years old, and it goes some way to gloss the Argentine's ruminations on chance, volume, absolute texts, and impossible libraries. In "The Universal Library," Lasswitz posits a computer-like "machine" invented by a mathematical genius. Like Huxley's deathless monkeys at their typewriters—that is, purely through the agency of chance—this machine is able to generate all the literature possible to mankind, including the spurious, the incomprehensible, the probable, and the manifestly improbable. The number of volumes projected by the genius inventor would reach ten to a power of two million ("simply 1 followed by 2 million zeros," as the "professor" observes). When the interlocutor objects that the professor has "calculated a library for which there is no room in the universe" (in German, *Raum* = room, *volume*, space), the professor does some number-chopping, and responds with a calculation that exploits both the spatial and textual senses of the term "volume" (*Volumen* in German and Spanish). In Willy Ley's translation:

> I assume you packed the library in 1000-volume boxes, each box having a capacity of precisely one cubic meter. All space to the furthest known spiral galaxies would not hold the Universal Library. In fact, you would need this volume of space so often that the number of packed universes would be a figure with only some 60 zeros less than the figure for the number of volumes.[20]

Through the window of mathematics, one sees how pitifully small the total production of world literature has become in this *Back to the Future* scenario: "The figure is not infinite," says the wizard of the machine, who has imagined a universe packed with tightly closed books. "The mathematics of it are flawless. What is surprising is that we can write down on a very small piece of paper the number of volumes comprising all possible literature."[21] In his own "Total Library," Borges isolates the source of the disturbance occasioned by the professor's flawless numbers: "Lasswitz urges mankind to construct that inhuman library which chance would organize and which would itself eliminate intelligence." Clearly Borges, the poet of volume and hypervolume, is the one to bring us out of mathematical hyperspace. "The painless and chaste extravagance of enormous numbers," he observes, "creates without a doubt that peculiar pleasure common to all excess" (*Borges, A Reader*, 66).

Borges's elegant essay, "The Enigma of Edward Fitzgerald" (1952) suggests a deep-seated, a-Platonic connection between philosophy, mathematics, and poetry, while the "Doctrine of Cycles" (1931) and the later essay on Spinoza (1967) demonstrate his familiarity with Georg Cantor's infinite *aleph*. "The Enigma" ponders the "collaboration" of the Victorian translator of the *Rubaiyat of Omar Khayyam* and the eleventh-century mathematician who first contrived its verses. Borges deftly sketches in what he wants the reader to know about Omar:

> He does not believe in astrology, but he cultivates astronomy, collaborates on the reform of the calendar . . . and writes a famous treatise on algebra, which gives numerical solutions for first- and second-degree equations, and geometric solutions—by the intersection of conics—for third-degree equations. (*Borges, A Reader*, 248)[22]

From geometric algebra and applied mathematics, Borges turns to Omar's theological studies and his production of verse:

> The arcana of numbers and stars do not exhaust his attention; in the solitude of his library he reads the texts of Plotinus. . . . He is an atheist, but he knows the orthodox interpretation of the Koran's most difficult passages, because every cultivated man is a theologian. . . . In the intervals between astronomy, algebra, and apologetics, Omar ben Ibrahim al Khayyami writes compositions of four lines whose first, second, and last lines rhyme; he has been credited with 500 of these quatrains. . . . (*Borges, A Reader*, 249)

In this succinct account, Borges catalogs Omar's intellectual pursuits from the observation of planetary motions to the solving of mathematical problems to the study of philosophy and a sacred text. "In the intervals" between serious pursuits, we are told, he entertains himself by constructing rhymed quatrains for which he will surely not be celebrated, "because in Persia . . . the poet must be prolific" and five hundred is "an exiguous number that will be unfavorable to his reputation." But the poetry of the *Rubaiyat* is precisely what Omar Khayyam is remembered for (by way of the "more sensitive and more sad" Fitzgerald), and this unmentioned but glaringly obvious fact may be one of the subtler ironies of the "Enigma." What one also discerns between the lines is Borges's empathy with the poet he describes—an intensely private man of varied gifts and far-flung interests.

From Omar to Nietzsche's Zarathustra is something of a leap, but Borges's "refutation" of the concept of Eternal Return in "The Doctrine of Cycles" (1934) places him squarely in the middle of late-nineteenth- and early-twentieth-century mathematics. Borges's footnote to this essay opposes a positivist frame of reference to Nietzsche's visionary writings. He cites Bertrand Russell's *Introduction to Mathematical Philosophy*, Russell's *ABC of Atoms*, and Eddington's *The Nature of the Physical World*, as well as various works by Nietzsche. Borges accomplishes his refutation of the Nietzschean doctrine by ranging against it nothing less than Georg Cantor's transfinite number theory—the most visionary construct in mathematics. David Hilbert, a leading mathematician of the early twentieth century, called it "one of the most beautiful realizations of human activity in the domain of the purely intelligible," and added, "No one shall expel us from the paradise which Cantor has created for us."[23] As we shall see, however, Cantor's transfinite "paradise" did not strike all mathematicians so favorably.

Joseph Warren Dauben points out in his fine biography, *Georg Cantor: His Mathematics and Philosophy of the Infinite*, that Cantorian set theory made it possible to deal successfully for the first time with the nature of mathematical infinity, a problematic area for mathematicians at the time. According to Dauben, Cantor began his studies of continuity and the infinite by relating number to a geometric continuum (i.e., each number in a series corresponded to a point in a line.) He then focused on number independently of "geometric isomorphisms," moved to a study of point sets, and the distinctions in force between discrete and continuous domains. Dauben sets forth Cantor's breakthrough to a mathematics of infinity, a solution that echoes all the way back to Archimedes' *Sand-reckoner*: "Declaring simply that sets with finite cardinal numbers were to be called finite sets, Cantor defined all others to be transfinite sets and their cardinals transfinite numbers."[24] (Boyer explains the naming: the "power" of a set became the "cardinal number" of the set, and an infinite set was called a "cardinal number" or "transfinite number.")[25] Dauben continues, "The first example of a transfinite cardinal number, then, was the power of the set of all finite cardinal numbers," which Cantor represented as *aleph null*, the first letter of the Hebrew alphabet followed by a subscript zero. The choice of symbol was especially felicitous, Dauben remarks, "since the Hebrew aleph served simultaneously to represent the number one, and the transfinite numbers, as cardinal numbers were themselves infinite unities."

Most simply put, "transfinite numbers" is the name given to the hierarchy of infinities defined by Cantor and designated by the succession of symbols beginning with *aleph null*. Each *aleph* (*aleph$_1$, aleph$_2$, aleph$_3$,* and so forth) is infinitely greater than the one immediately preceding it, while the first transfinite number—the *aleph null (aleph$_0$)*—corresponds to the infinity we ordinarily speak of when we use the term. In Cantorian theory, just as there are infinitely many natural numbers, so also are there infinitely many transfinite numbers. For Borges's story, "The Aleph," two things only need to be kept in mind: A Cantorian transfinite "set" is actually an infinite *series*—whether it is called a "set" or a "transfinite number," or a "cardinal number"; and Cantor's "aleph" is an *infinite unity*.

Cantor's revolutionary theorems were subject to savage criticism by contemporaries, because of (says Boyer) "considerable *horror infiniti*" among mathematicians. His transfinite arithmetic was counterintuitive, "a beautiful example of a mathematical paradox, of a true statement that seems false to the uninformed."[26] In 1892, the great logician and mathematician, Gottlob Frege, called the concept of mathematical infinity the issue over which mathematics would be wrecked: "Here is the reef on which it will founder. For the infinite will eventually refuse to be excluded from arithmetic and yet it is irreconcilable with [a finitist, positivist] epistemological approach."[27] Cantor's approach to the infinite precipitated what Einstein later called "the fiercest 'frog-mouse' battle in mathematical history."[28] At the time, however, repeated attacks by Cantor's highly respected contemporary, Leopold Kronecker, seem to have exacerbated Cantor's tendency to depression and contributed to a series of nervous breakdowns; he died in a mental hospital. In context, we can note that Cantor (1845–1918) is precisely contemporary with Nietzsche (1844–1900) who also was "hounded for his ideas and went beyond the bounds of reason," as a note to Borges's essay, "The Doctrine of Cycles, " informs us. (*Borges, A Reader*, 345).

In "The Doctrine of Cycles," Borges ranges Cantor's transfinite sets against Nietzsche's doctrine of eternal return. He begins by outlining the atomist theory underlying "the most terrible idea in the universe":

> The number of all the atoms which make up the world is, although
> excessive, finite, and as such only capable of a finite . . . number of

permutations. Given an infinite length of time, the number of possible permutations must be exhausted, and the universe must repeat itself. Once again you will be born of the womb, once again you will live all the hours until the hour of your incredible death. Such is the customary order of the argument . . . usually attributed to Nietzsche. (*Borges, A Reader*, 65–66)

In a brilliant move, Borges now counters the notion of a finite universe by appealing to "Georg Cantor and his heroic theory of aggregates," that is, the endlessly proliferating infinitudes—the "powers"—of transfinite number theory:

Cantor destroys the foundation of Nietzsche's thesis. He affirms the perfect infinity of the number of points in the universe, and even of a meter of the universe or a fraction of that meter. (*Borges, A Reader*, 66)

Borges goes on to expound Cantorian infinite sets (*Mengenlehre*) with a crystalline simplicity. I will quote him at some length, for while Borges silently weaves these concepts into his fiction, he defines them in his essays. He begins: "An infinite collection—for instance, the natural series of whole numbers—is a collection whose members can split off into infinite series." Next, he explains the technical meaning of "well ordered": "The series of natural numbers is well ordered; in other words, the terms which form it are consecutive: 28 precedes 29 and follows 27." Now he can approach the concept of transfinite number, which he sets forth in terms comparable to Zeno's infinite regress: "But the series of points in space (or of moments in time) cannot be ordered in the same way. No number has an immediate successor or predecessor . . . like the series of fractions according to magnitude. What fraction shall we enumerate after 1/2? Not 51/100, because 101/200 is closer; not 101/200 because 201/400 is closer. . . . The same thing happens with points, according to Georg Cantor. We can always insert others in infinite numbers" (*Borges, A Reader*, 67). Borges is explaining with great clarity that, in Cantor's mathematics, the series that occurs *between* zero and one is as infinite as any series that *follows* from one.

What seems to exert the strongest fascination for Borges is the counterintuitive relation, in Cantorian set theory, of the part to the whole. An infinite set, he points out, is defined as "that set which can equal one of its partial sets," and he illustrates the exact sense of this proposition: "In these elevated latitudes of enumeration, the part is no less copious than the whole; *the exact quantity of points in the universe is the same as in a meter, or in a decimeter, or in the farthest stellar trajectory"* (my italics). Borges returns again and again in his writings to the equinumerosity, the uncanny commensurability, of cosmic and microcosmic domains. He concludes his argument in "The Doctrine of Cycles" with the satisfaction of a chess player announcing checkmate: "This brush of Cantor's lovely game with Zarathustra's lovely game is fatal for Zarathustra. If the universe consists of an infinite number of terms then it is equally capable of an infinite number of combinations, and the need for a recurrence is invalidated."

Cantor's "lovely game" becomes a way for Borges to talk about the "inconceivably infinite" God of Baruch Spinoza ("I don't mean very numerous, I mean infinite") and, in a lighter register, one finds Cantorian sets and subsets supplying the framework for one of the more playful parodies of the composite critic, "Bustos Domecq." In the late essay on Spinoza (1967), Borges summons up Cantor's *aleph null* series to dramatically illustrate the meaning of "infinite": "In Georg Cantor's mathematics, a transfinite number is one in which the parts are not less than the whole; Cantor demonstrates this with three infinite series. The first consists of all the whole numbers; we begin with one, we continue with two, three, and four, and we, and all the generations of the future, will die before reaching the end of the series."[29] Having killed off the human race to make his point, Borges tackles the second series (1, 3, 5, etc.) and the third (2, 4, 6, etc.) and observes, "[I]f we take the series of whole numbers minus hundreds of millions, what remains is still infinite. This is the way Spinoza saw his God, as strictly infinite." Borges has honored the philosopher's rational approach to the Deity and the humility of his daily work in his poem, "Spinoza":

> Free of metaphor and myth, he grinds
> a stubborn crystal: the infinite
> map of the One who is all his stars.
>
> (*Borges, A Reader*, 285)

"Bustos Domecq" is the stylish, somewhat contemptuous, highly opinionated literary critic, a persona developed by Borges in conjunction with his collaborator in mischief, Adolfo Bioy Casares. The historic Cantor and the fictional Domecq are character models for the narrator of "The Aleph." One of the parodies developed by Bioy Casares and Borges for the collected criticism of Domecq is a small pearl entitled "The Brotherhood Movement." Cantorian set theory is turned to use in this essay to spoof the ubiquitous phenomenon of the men's club, among other "sets" of things. Recorded are a shifting "multitude of secret societies, or brotherhoods, whose members are not only unknown to each other" but who may "at any given moment, change their status."[30] There is no "smart set" in Domecq's catalog of unwitting fraternities, which includes those who "at this very moment, in Brazil or Africa, are inhaling the odor of jasmine or, more culture-minded and studious, reading a bus ticket." Subspecies take root and spread rhizomically (to use Umberto Eco's classification of the "rhizomic labyrinth").[31] Included in the constantly narrowing subsets of the Brotherhood Movement are "persons attacked by a cigarette cough who, at the same time, may also be wearing baggy trousers or be sprinting on ten-speed bicycles or be riding the New York Times Square Shuttle." Inevitably, this parody of set theoretics implodes, as it were, in a Borgesian *regressus ad absurdum*: "Think . . . of the present brotherhood of persons who are thinking about labyrinths; of those who, a minute ago forgot; of those who two minutes ago forgot; of those who four and a half; of those who five. . . ." (authors' ellipses).[32]

Even in parody, Borges has slipped from modern set theory back to Zeno's immortal construct of Achilles and the Tortoise as though he were traveling an ideational Möbius strip. Kramer helps to explain this phenomenon. Citing philosophers and mathematicians who have given serious thought to the Eleatic's paradoxes against motion—Aquinas, Descartes, Leibnitz, Spinoza, and Bergson—she generalizes: "Zeno's paradoxes in some form have been used as arguments for all the theories of space, time, and infinity that have been propounded from his day to ours."[33] Contemporary logicians bring terms such as "limit" and "convergence" to the concepts of finitude and infinitude, but still use the "Z" or "Zeno" series to indicate the mathematical concept of infinite regression.[34] Borges follows Lewis Carroll, along with more august philosophers and mathematicians, into the same labyrinth.

"The Aleph"

Je le vois, mais je ne le crois pas
—Cantor to Dedekind, 1877

Borges's tale, "The Aleph," centers around a vision in darkness that encompasses infinity and contains a crucial episode of enumeration. Among the mathematical concepts that can be recognized in "The

Aleph," apart from Cantorian set theory, are oppositions of *identity* and *identicality, probability* as a calculus of alternate realities, and *commutativity*, or Abelian mirroring, i.e., the rule governing the exchangeability of elements in a given arithmetic or algebraic context [6 x 9 = 9 x 6]. As in other Borges tales, one finds key geometric emblems and a certain amount of letter/number play.

"The Aleph" figures as a romance in both senses of the term; that is, it recounts an adventure and explores the psychology of an unrequited passion. The story is told in the first person. It begins with a woman's death, develops the antagonism of a pair of literary men, climaxes in a powerful visionary experience, and ends with a house destroyed. The narrator, a poet and critic, pays periodic visits to the home of his dead beloved, Beatriz Viterbo, whose memory he obsessively cherishes although she refused his attentions with a stony heart. Her snobbish cousin, Carlos Argentino Danieri (initials CAD), reveals to the narrator his ambitious poetic venture—a baroque epic entitled *The Earth*. The grandly titled poem turns out to be pompous and contrived, a monumental bore, but the grieving lover welcomes the opportunity to spend time in the house which still displays photographs of Beatriz.[35] The two men cordially detest one another but are drawn ever closer, as much from competitiveness and spite as from shared interests and after-dinner brandy. When he discovers that his landlords, Zunino and Zungri, plan to demolish the family home—unless the lawyer Zunni thwarts the enterprise—Danieri reveals to the visitor his secret of secrets: the Aleph in the cellar. We note, in passing, the juxtaposition of the three busy Z's to the transcendental Aleph, "one of those points in space that contains all other points," we are told, and "the only place on earth where all places are—seen from every angle."[36]

The narrator, who names himself "Borges" as he communes with the icon of Beatriz, allows himself to be taken to the cellar by Danieri. He is placed on his back, told to focus on the nineteenth step, and left in the dark. He suddenly realizes Danieri may be insane and fears murder; but at this moment he spots the Aleph—"a small iridescent sphere of almost intolerable brilliance"—and experiences a profoundly moving vision. Danieri shocks him out of his enchantment with trivializing verbal jabs, and the narrator takes his revenge by refusing to acknowledge what he has seen. At the end, it is Danieri whose revenge is nearly complete: his dreadful poem has netted second prize, and "Borges," who has won nothing, is left to lick his wounds. The house on Garay Street is destroyed, and with it, access to the Aleph. We arrive at the "Postscript of March first, 1943," in which the narrator cites sources for the term *aleph* in a dry academic manner and, strangely, repudiates his vision. He declares the Aleph of Garay Street to have been a "false Aleph," because he has learned that the true one exists "in the heart of a stone" *(en lo íntimo de una piedra)*. We are left wondering which of the two men is really mad, and puzzled as to what the Aleph really signifies.

Do the mathematical aspects of the story shed light on these questions? We need to call up the Dantean framework of the story to recognize their significance, for it is not only the true Aleph that exists within a stone but the heart of Beatriz Viterbo and the heart of her forerunner, Dante's Beatrice of the *Vita Nuova*. Monegal usefully reads "The Aleph" as a "parodic reduction of the Divine Comedy" and suggests that the "process of miniaturization and the outrageous level on which the parody works are so radical that many readers miss the obvious clues contained in Beatriz Viterbo's name, in Carlos Argentino Danieri's insane poem, and in 'Borges's' quest, which leads him to the vision of the Aleph (Dante's microcosm) in the cellar of an old Buenos Aires house."[37]

Dante's numerological structuring of the *Commedia* was clearly not lost on Borges, who chose alphanumerical titles for both of his parables drawn from it—*Inferno, I, 32* and *Paradiso, XXXI, 108*. Monegal further points out that the name "Danieri" in "The Aleph" is simply a telescoping of "Dante Alighieri." However, it is the character "Borges" who experiences the cosmic vision (although Danieri has clearly experienced similar visions), and it is Borges, in reality, whose blindness—or visual exile within his own city—parallels Dante's enforced absence, in all but memory, from the beloved Florence. In fact, both Danieri *and* "Borges" may be identified with Dante, which helps to explain the curiously fluid *identity exchange* that takes place in "The Aleph"—not only between the two characters, but between the two characters and their author. This interchange supplies one of the links between language and mathematics so characteristic of Borges's fiction. In "The Aleph," Borges has turned two mathematical principles—algebraic "identity" and the Abelian "commutative law"—to literary use.

The lexicon defines *identity* as "being the same in all qualities under consideration." An alternative meaning is "being some specific person or thing; individuality." That is, with the flexibility possible to language, the term can denote duplication or singularity, similitude or unique existence—the choice of meaning is determined by context. In mathematics, an *identity* generally refers to an "identical equation," that is, an algebraic equation $(x + y = y + x)$ that may be satisfied by giving any values whatever to the literal quantities ("literal" in this case signifying "letter"). We understand by this that when exact values are assigned to x and y, it can be shown that both terms of the equation are the same. They represent identical values; the logician's "A is A." All these aspects of identity meet in "The Aleph," but the mathematical sense is predominant. The story contains two topical centers (above, below) and maintains a balance between two centers of consciousness—"Borges" and "Danieri"—like the two terms of an equation. While these men are shown from the outset to be social and aesthetic "equivalents," the critic "Borges" and the poet "Danieri" end up with identical values. In addition, we see that Borges has chosen for his major characters "given" names with initials that suggest the letter-quantities used in algebra: C, A, and B (apart from the three busy Z's).

What I have referred to as "topical centers"—that is, the crucial moment in the house *above* and the crucial passage in the basement *below*—reinforces the calculus of double identity. The episode in the drawing room employs cumulative, repeated naming and finally reveals the "identity" of the narrator. The reader becomes a voyeur, like Danieri, as his guest addresses the portrait of the dead woman: "Beatriz, Beatriz Elena, Beatriz Elena Viterbo, darling Beatriz, Beatriz now gone forever, it's me, it's Borges." Like Dante, Borges becomes a character in his own work; and following Dante, the dead Beatriz is internalized by the character "Borges" as an obsession. The second episode occurs in another kind of hallucinarium. The topical center shifts to the cellar below *(sótano)* where "Borges" silently submits to his antagonist's point of view, seeing the universe as it were through Danieri's eyes. As "Borges" experiences Carlos Argentino's *Aleph*, their two identities momentarily merge, only to spring apart at the next encounter. Or do they spring apart?

In "The Aleph," Borges mercilessly caricatures his own literary personae. Both "Borges" and "Danieri" are poets and critics. Both conform to their author's idea of the worst kind of literary parasite; both maintain the megalomaniac pedantry and contemptuous attitude of "Bustos Domecq," the hypercritic. Significantly, the "second prize" that Danieri is awarded for his dreadful book of poems reflects the second prize that Borges actually received, in 1929, for *his* third book of poems. Danieri and "Borges," both, are representations of Jorge Luis Borges— poet, critic, essayist, lecturer, storyteller—and their conflict emerges as a species of identity crisis.

In mathematics, and in logic, the "commutative law" states that the *order* in which elements of certain operations are given is immaterial. We accept as obvious the concept that digits can change places while their sum remains the same ($9 \times 3 = 3 \times 9$). Similarly, in "The Aleph," we discover that while certain operations (adding, taking away) are in force, characters change places without changing the results: "Borges" is unseated and Danieri unhoused. By the end of the story, "Borges," the once admired and sought-after critic, has yielded his place to the triumphant, prize-winning Danieri. Nothing else has changed; the poetry is still bad, and Beatriz is still dead. The revelation in the cellar has been denied and trivialized, while the unhappy, almost toneless voice of the "Postscript" is ambiguous in the extreme. We know it is "Borges" who speaks, but it might as easily be Danieri, depressed by the loss of his house and his *Aleph*. Indeed, the closing sentence of the late essay, "Borges and I," would beautifully supply "The Aleph" with its own closing line: "I do not know which of us has written this page."[38]

The exchange of dialogue that takes place in the cellar suggests also an *exchange of personal identities*. This "commutation" is realized when the humiliated "Borges" revenges himself on Danieri by his deliberate refusal to acknowledge the *Aleph*—and so insinuates the other's insanity. At this point, the pure lover of Beatriz has become a pure hater of Danieri. His tone and manner change radically, and remain changed right through the "Postscript." In the end, "Borges" has taken on Danieri's unpleasant manner and way of thinking. He now embodies the object of his contempt; he has changed places with his antagonist. Or has he gone quite mad?

As in the case of the priest Tzinacán's mystical vision in "The God's Script," the reader must wonder whether Borges's character, "Borges," has been vouchsafed a spiritual revelation or suffered a hallucination. Or if, repeating the history of Georg Cantor, he has traveled from creative vision to unalloyed insanity. This latter possibility draws the narrator of "The Aleph" into a meaningful triangulation with both Dante and Cantor. The history of Cantor's war with Kronecker and his eventual breakdown serves to anchor Borges's account of closely linked antagonists in actual reality: "Kronecker continued his attacks on the hypersensitive and temperamental Cantor, and in 1884 Cantor suffered the first of the nervous breakdowns that were to recur throughout the remaining thirty-three years of his life. . . . his death in a mental institution in Halle is a reminder that genius and madness are sometimes related."[39] The fine line between genius and madness is, as we know, a Borgesian theme dating back to "The South" and to Borges's actual experience of delirium that the story memorializes. But although we cannot be certain as to whether the vision of "The Aleph" denotes delirium or clairvoyance, we can usefully address three aspects: the focus on the nineteenth step; its "chaotic" catalog of images; and the symmetrical figure of the spiderweb in the pyramid. All three convey a mathematical dimension of meaning.

The vision at the nineteenth step carries us to the heart of the story. But why *nineteen*? No numerological significance attaches to it as, for example, it does to eighteen—the Hebrew number/letter symbol meaning "life"—or to unlucky seventeen. In the darkness of the cellar with the trapdoor shut, "Borges" focuses on the nineteenth step and then perceives the Aleph. The story hinges on this moment. The narrator points to it as the "ineffable center" of his tale. The number nineteen, therefore, functions as a springboard that projects narrator (and reader) out of ordinary space-time and into a multiplex dimension of extraordinary clarity and specificity. If "Borges's" reference in the "Postscript" to Cantor can be used as a guide, an explanation suggests itself. For Borges's nineteenth step calls up Cantor's solution to a problem that, in its own way, recalls the Cabalists' problem of joining a finite earth with an infinite deity.

Cantor's creation of the first transfinite cardinal number established a passageway to mathematical infinity. The term "cardinal" derives from Latin *cardinalis*, meaning "hinge" or "pivot," and as Dauben tells us, the "aleph null" set became "the pivotal element between the finite and infinite domains."[40] We recall too that Cantor solved the problem of connecting the two domains by defining *the first transfinite cardinal number as the power of the set of all cardinal numbers.*[41] "Borges's" vision of the Aleph takes place on a staircase, which symbolically parallels Cantor's ascending series of transfinite numbers, just as it can represent the incremental increase of natural numbers. But it is the linking of finite and infinite domains by the agency of the *cardinal numbers* that suggests why Borges chose to locate his Aleph at, specifically, the nineteenth step. It has to do with where *finite* cardinal numbers may be said to begin and end.

With the addition of the zero, our entire arithmetic—a decimal system of whole integers—is founded on the digits one through nine. Just as the operations of language are confined to twenty-six letters in our alphabet system, so do the operations of arithmetic take place within the limits of the ten number symbols. Borges introduces the vision of the Aleph by observing: "All language is an alphabet of symbols whose use presupposes a past shared by all other interlocutors." In the community of symbols, one and nine are the alpha and omega of number; between these two digits lies the entire set of symbols that constitute our counting system, the "alphabet of symbols" that represent the cardinal numbers. All the digits except zero are collapsed within the number "nineteen." The numbers may proliferate and "all the generations of the future may die before reaching the end of the series," as Borges put it, but nineteen—and only nineteen—bookends the entire set of symbols for the cardinal numbers. The nineteenth step, then, representing the totality of the finite cardinal numbers, becomes a launching pad: It indicates *the point of departure from the finite to the infinite*. Cantor moves from the finite and denumerable, to the infinite and denumerable, to the transfinite nondenumerable cardinals. Borges could not have chosen a more significant number—nor did he forget the zero, the algorist holding place that completes the system. The Aleph itself corresponds to the zero. His "small iridescent sphere, of almost intolerable brilliance," encompassing the myriad aspects of the microcosm, corresponds to the magical "holding place" that opens up infinite possibilities of enumeration. Which brings us to the "chaotic enumeration" of the vision itself.

Monegal states that Borges has attempted "in the short space of two pages what Dante (very wisely) refused to do in the conclusion of his *Comedy*: to describe the ineffable," and outlines his method: "Using the Whitmanesque device of anaphora [rhetorical repetition of an opening phrase], Borges, in order to describe a point in space which simultaneously contains all points in space and time, resorts to a dazzling and chaotic enumeration."[42] Monegal's reading of "The Aleph" is genuinely helpful, but it seems to me that Borges has been remarkably successful in conveying the ineffable at this crucial point; and further, it is precisely his "dazzling and chaotic enumeration" that works the fictional magic. The effect is powerful, however, because Borges's rhetorical device employs a letter/number operator that *systematically* projects the disparate images across the threshold of what cannot be said.

Borges selects images for the vision that seem to wrench space and time apart, for they themselves are wrenched apart violently in space and time—fragmented scenes both personal and impersonal, primordial and contemporary, seen from all perspectives, as in a cubist universe. These "facets" of the vision include a Homeric "heavy-laden sea," the cancer in a Scotswoman's breast, an antique Persian instrument of measure, "all the ants on earth," the shadows of delicate ferns, people in the act of love, and—horribly—the "atrocious relic of what had been Beatriz Viterbo." Simultaneously, "Borges" sees the composite whole and the singular part: "convex deserts and every grain of sand in them." Most terrible perhaps, if we recall the motive that drives him to Danieri's house, "Borges" sees in a desk drawer "obscene, incredible, precise letters, which Beatriz had written Carlos Argentino." This hint of an incestuous bond, coupled with the shocking sight of Beatriz's decayed remains *(reliquia atroz)* may well have induced the lover's revulsion— and the denial of knowledge—that results in the postscript's insistence on a "false Aleph."

The "chaotic enumeration" that structures the vision is a variant of the epic catalog, an ancient trope that Borges uses frequently. For example, his verses on "Matthew, 25: 30" (1953) set forth a seemingly disconnected enumeration, his "feeble translation . . . of what was a single limitless Word":

> Stars, bread, libraries of East and West,
> playing cards, chessboards, galleries, skylights, cellars
> a human body to walk with on earth,
> fingernails, growing at nighttime and in death,
> shadows for forgetting, mirrors which endlessly multiply,
> falls in music, gentlest of all time's shapes,
> borders of Brazil, Uruguay, horses and mornings,
> a bronze weight, a copy of Grettir Saga,
> algebra and fire. . . .

The visionary catalog of "The Aleph" also calls up algebra and fire: the embers of a fiery passion, and "algebra" in the sense of letter symbols that represent numbers. The "numbering" aspect derives from the anaphoric repetition of "I saw," the phrase that introduces each image or scene. "I saw" is the translation of *vi* in the original Spanish, and here we may have uncovered an intuitive synthesis of letter and number that cannot carry over in translation. In the original "El Aleph," the term *vi* occurs thirty-nine times in the passage recording the vision, and it is immediately evident that the verb of vision, first person, past tense, replicates the roman numeral "six." Borges certainly knew that six is the first "perfect" number—i.e., equal to the sum of all its factors except itself (as $6 = 1 + 2 + 3$). Although one might extend this idea to the Aleph, I am not suggesting a "numerological" meaning to the *vi* as a perfect number, but the possibility that the word/number association is significant in itself. In this passage the syntax effects a precise partitioning, and the operator or agent of the compartmentalization is the repetition of an identical term. Grammar is establishing a "calculus" of visionary images. Like the development of a complex fugue, the episodic scenes of the vision are structured on a stable mathematical format. One must ask if the ecstatic quality that attaches to "Borges's" vision, the sense of rapture that surrounds it, would be as forcefully conveyed were it not so concretely structured. The *vi* is one articulation, in Borges's world, of the intimate relations between word and number, which at times become "one flesh."

Four rather severe images interpenetrate the highly wrought fabric of the vision. Taking them in turn, "Borges" sees the Aleph itself, a "point in space"; then, a pyramid with a cobweb at its center; a "terraqueous globe between two mirrors that multiplied it endlessly" (a grotesque echo of the scriptural "world without end"); and finally, an astrolabe, a device used to measure the distance of the earth from the sun and stars. These images order the vision in another way. There is a geometric expansion from a sphere measuring two or three centimeters to a monumental polyhedron, to a planetary image "multiplied endlessly." The astrolabe suggests invisible radii connecting the "terraqueous" planet to the most distant galaxies. The enumeration of the various images is certainly chaotic, as it turns out, but methodically diversified. By way of its emblems, the vision has been subject to strict geometric structuring. The immense spatial expansions implied by the series of emblems carry the visionary experience from the densely packed microcosm to the realm of the finite to the limitless reaches of the universe.

While only the Aleph itself—the "sphere whose center is everywhere"—signifies the action of something divinely beyond human control *(significar la divinidad)*, each of the four emblems pairs human technology together with design found in nature. Of them all, the "silvery spiderweb at the center of a black pyramid" *(plateada telaraña en el centro de una negra pirámide)* most effectively conjoins the technologies of man and nature. It represents the ephemeral attached to the enduring, the pyramid constructed to last forever, the web spun daily with the rising of the sun. It says something about creaturely persistence in time. The image contains no living thing, only the wondrous remains of man and spider—or, perhaps the remains of male and female architectures, both linked with death. The luminous filaments of arachnid radii, the polygons and trapezoids that lead to the central waiting room, contrast sharply with the massive polygons and triangles of the great stone tombs. But the emblem of pyramid and web also functions as a kind of bookplate, a graphic *ars poetica*. It can be seen as the key emblem that encodes the message sent by the story as a whole.

Its black and silver coloration underscores the funereal aspects of the tomb and the trap; it also suggests the realm of dreams and the world of the blind. But this particular emblem connects the author with "Borges," his character, in yet another way. In 1943, Borges published a collection of his poetry—*Poemas, 1922–1943*—illustrated on the cover by an angel cutting a diamond which is set in a cobweb, almost the precise reverse of the key emblem of "The Aleph."[43] "The Aleph" was published six years later, in 1949. In the story, the graphic reversal of the cover image of Borges's successful publication of poems, symbolically reflects the rejected, unproductive, unsuccessful condition of the character, "Borges." The device thus invokes the principle of the part that is "not less than the whole." Moreover, it provides a key to the lethal nature of romance in this tale.

In the most direct reading, the spiderweb at the heart of the pyramid pictures a trap for the living set within a tomb for the dead. It depicts the abode of necrophilia. It captures in a spare geometric image—a construct of planes, angles, tangents—the love story of "Borges" and Beatriz. In a master-stroke, the emblem creates the space of a living death, appropriate to the narrator's tale of mounting negations—unrequited passion, erotic obsession, unresolved ambition, personal humiliation and, at the end, a submerged identity. At the most literal level, the geometric emblem shows the seductive web of power relations contained within the triangle CBB, the love-hate triangle that remains in force between Carlos Argentino, Beatriz, and "Borges," all three occupants—or inmates—of Jorge Luis Borges's own hallucinarium, "The Aleph."

6

"Ten Minutes for Seven Letters":
Beloved

How do you account for the slaughter of a beloved infant? How do you deal with slavery, death camps, prison camps? How do you explain the brutalization of an entire people? How do you handle genocide?—*Sixty Million / and more*. Can such experience be articulated? And if words fail to tell, what can numbers say?

Toni Morrison's novel, *Beloved*, brought her the Pulitzer Prize for fiction in 1988 and a virtual avalanche of praise—with the exception of one sour reviewer who trivialized the bold and powerful new work as a second-rate piece of feminist propaganda. Since then, the novel has attracted a good deal of critical attention. Approaches have focused on its "Gothic" and folkloric aspects, hinged upon slave narrative, black history, and systems of community, examined the pathology of mother-daughter relations, and drawn parallels with classical tragedy—specifically with *Medea*.[1] Style-oriented readers have remarked on the deft commingling of realism and allegory in Morrison's work, the linguistic richness of her dialectic, and the poetry of her lyric voice. Margaret Atwood cited "the magnificent practicality" with which Morrison treated the supernatural element, and characterized the novel's dialectical interweavings with beautiful accuracy as "antiminimalist prose that is by turns rich, graceful, eccentric, rough, lyrical, sinuous [and] colloquial."[2] But *Beloved* was never an "easy read."

Morrison's narrative style in the novel—disjointed, chronologically inverted, "allusive and oblique," as one reader termed it—performs two functions. On the one hand, the disjointed narrative mimetically suggests the "fractured" recall of patients who have suffered clinical trauma. One of the earliest critiques recognized the "splintered, piecemeal revelation of the past" as part of the technical virtuosity of the

113

work. We gradually understand, Walter Clemens noted, "that this isn't tricky storytelling but the intricate exploration of trauma."[3] On the other hand, the twisting, multivoiced, achronological narrative allows Morrison to "avoid the excessive melodrama that a more straightforward form would have produced," as Philip Page has pointed out.[4] "The narrative fragmentation denies readers the expected level of comprehension," says Page, "and forces them to wait for explanations, to remember previously narrated fragments, and to piece together the narrative's chronology." The reader-turned-detective must gather evidence simply to understand what is going on. Morrison is forcing the reader to think about what happened one hundred years ago, and what is continuing to happen, whether the reader is male or female, black or white. At the same time, the narrative encourages identification with a damaged protagonist. From this perspective, the delaying and retarding of a too-easy pathos elicits the most profound experience of drama— the full emotional response that attends full comprehension. I want to examine Morrison's use of number, name, and color in the same frame of reference, as narrative instruments that encode information while enjoining restraint, that function precisely to avoid excessive— trivializing—melodrama.

From the very beginning, Morrison's novel handles explosive emotional material. It sets out to record the suffering, endurance, heroism, and horror, not at the level of a single protagonist alone but also—incredibly—at levels of gender, family, community, and race. In *Beloved*, the controlling and restraining effect of number is strongly evident. As in the chiseled works of Borges, letter and number may algebraically exchange functions; and, as in other of Morrison's novels, the names of people and places are carefully chosen to convey complex information. Finally, Morrison deploys color with extraordinary versatility: as abstract value, as aesthetic value, as dramatic shading, as societal division, to denote plenitude or dearth, or to signal annihilation. Toward the close of the novel, for example, Paul D stands in a doorway and finds that "in the place where once a shaft of sad red light had bathed him . . . is nothing. A bleak and minus nothing."[5] Morrison's "logistics" of color, number, and naming is calculated to set boundaries, to suggest unplumbable depths, to contain the uncontainable—in short, to hold the "unspeakable" firmly to its narrative course. Bringing form to a chaotic narrative, these structuring elements permit the reader to experience the grotesque events of the action with a peculiar intensity.

The melancholy Baby Suggs meditates on color as a philosopher would—qua color, as an abstract value. In her life, every spiritual certainty has been destroyed, every good act undone. "Since she knew death was anything but forgetfulness, she used the little energy left her for pondering color" (4). Perhaps at times she ponders color in the sense of the old conundrum: "Do you and I see different colors although we both call what we see 'red'"? White? Black? When I look at a white person, do I see the same thing that white people see? When white people look at a black person, do they see what I see? Wittgenstein, probing the nature of certainty, rather than the problem of perception, says: "Someone asks me: What is the colour of this flower? I answer: 'red'.— Are you absolutely sure? Yes, absolutely sure! But may I not have been deceived and called the wrong colour 'red'? No. The certainty with which I call the colour 'red' is the rigidity of my measuring rod."[6] Color is an equally rigid measuring rod in *Beloved*, and Baby Suggs has one philosophical certainty with respect to color comparable to Wittgenstein's restricted sense: *white means trouble*. Bloodred, of course, is the last color the dying grandmother of the ghost-babe wants to contemplate. "Bring a little lavender in, if you got any," she tells Sethe, "Pink, if you don't." And, we are told, "Sethe would oblige her with anything from fabric to her own tongue" (4).

We are continually reminded of the need for color. The opening pages of *Beloved* tell of a "gray and white house" set in an equally colorless landscape: "Winter in Ohio was especially rough if you had an appetite for color. Sky provided the only drama, and counting on a Cincinnati horizon for life's principal joy was reckless indeed" (4). Denver first sees "Beloved" as a spectral "white dress holding its arm around her mother's waist" (35). The baby ghost climbs up "lightning-white stairs" (13). Sethe explains why Baby Suggs is so starved for color in the house on Bluestone Road: "There wasn't any except for two orange squares in a quilt that made the absence shout" (38). We are introduced to Sethe's history by way of color: "[T]he last color she remembered was the pink chips in the headstone of her baby girl," and Sethe recognizes the escaped Paul D by his "peachtone skin" and straight back (7). It seems evident that color (used as symbol, for aesthetic "shading," abstraction, or literal description) is underscored in Morrison's text, not merely to indicate the figurative need for "some color" in one's life but because color—color people can see and react to—is what this book is about. But what kind of story does it tell?

From a distance, *Beloved* has the configuration of a series of concentric circles, and the motion of a whirlpool. At its center, a primal murder; immediately surrounding the murder, a wider context of slave-hunting and slave-killing; encircling both, the unchronicled history of the

Middle Passage, the slave ships, terror, hunger, disease, suicide, the sale of human beings for labor and breeding, the wrenching apart of families, and the ultimate bestialization of a people. All these elements resonate in a narrative distinguished by chaste restraint.

The tale begins in Ohio and spans a period of eighteen years, 1855 to 1873, bracketing the Civil War (which is never directly mentioned). It sporadically recounts events set in three locations: a Kentucky farm ironically named "Sweet Home"; a Georgia prison; and a haunted house on the outskirts of Cincinnati. To outline briefly: The story is about Sethe who, eighteen years earlier, had escaped from the Sweet Home farm during her sixth month of pregnancy. She gives birth with the help of a young white runaway—Amy Denver, for whom she names the newborn baby—and is ferried across the Ohio River to free territory. Arriving at her husband's mother's house, she rejoins her three older children and experiences a month of happiness—twenty-eight days, to be exact, or "the travel of one whole moon—of unslaved life" (95)—before she finds herself alienated from the neighboring black community, and discovers that Schoolteacher, the slave owner, has tracked her down. With a chain saw, she cuts the throat of her two-year-old daughter as he enters the woodshed.

The house becomes the haunting site of a baby poltergeist who emerges, finally, as "Beloved," a flesh-and-blood visitant, a young woman who increasingly takes control of the home and destroys its peace and its very life until a compassionate gathering of community women exorcise the demonic influence. Woven into the narrative from the very first chapter is the story of "Paul D," who has undergone imprisonment and suffered excruciating and emasculating experiences since leaving "Sweet Home." He comes to live with Sethe and brings her affection and strength, but is first seduced and then forced out of the house by a jealous "Beloved" who continues to batten on the mother. We are left at the end with a banished ghost, a wasted Sethe, a returned Paul D, a living daughter who has moved out into the community, and an open-ended question as to the outcome. The whole is told in flashes of "rememory," a painful process of recall.

From end to end, we find Morrison using symbols the way a poet does. These are not confined to visual emblems, such as the "tree" engraved by whiplash on Sethe's back, but include number and color. We are located from the outset at an address composed of number and color: 124 Bluestone Road. In "Unspeakable Things Unspoken: The Afro-American Presence in American Literature," Morrison comments on the symbolic significance of the numerals:

Beginning *Beloved* with numerals rather than spelled out numbers, it was my intention to give the house an identity separate from the street or even the city; to name it the way "Sweet Home" was named ... but not with nouns or "proper" names—with numbers instead because numbers have no adjectives, no posture of coziness or grandeur. . . .[7]

But one is also meant to be deliberately *dislocated* by the abrupt, hardly intelligible opening sentence: *124 was spiteful.* As Morrison puts it, "The reader is snatched, yanked, thrown into an environment completely foreign, snatched just as the slaves were from one place to another, without preparation and without defense."[8] This chaotic initiation into the life of the novel is modified, in retrospect, by the symmetry of its framework, the stability of its triangular structures.

The architecture of *Beloved* follows a Dantean triadic model. Morrison has designed the novel in three separate sections, each of which opens with a three-word sentence establishing a mood: *124 was spiteful; 124 was loud; 124 was quiet.* "Numbers here constitute an address," Morrison amplifies, "a thrilling enough prospect for slaves who owned nothing, least of all an address."[9] The address on Bluestone Road presents a sequence of three cardinal numbers—one, two, and four—from which "three" itself is conspicuously absent. Included in Morrison's structural design is the trio of major characters, a satiric parallel of the male Trinity in the persons of Mother, Daughter, and Unholy Ghost—which seems related, somehow, to the presence of visible and invisible "threes."

One senses a Dantean economy as well, a suggestion of being moved through zodiacal "houses" by the numerical openings with their single modal change: "changes from spiteful to loud to quiet, as the sounds in the body of the ship itself may have changed," notes Morrison, relating the progress of the story to the journey in slave ships.[10] The story line, in fact, describes a grotesque reversal of the Dantean journey, just as Morrison's trinity of women "reverses" the construct of Father, Son, and Holy Ghost. Sethe, the protagonist of *Beloved*, travels from Edenic ignorance at "Sweet Home" to the dark river-crossing with "Stamp Paid" as Charon, to the brief existence in "holy" Baby Suggs's earthly paradise, to the sacrificial slaying that is both damnation and salvation, through an interminable purgatory where one deals with gnawing guilt. Sethe, however, does not have to finally *arrive* at the infernal region. From the beginning of the story, hell is all around her and always has been.

We are in a position, now, to consider the two-sided instrument by which Morrison draws the reader into the region of the unspeakable: the strategic use of number to encode meaning, and the intuitive use of number to contain feeling. To do this, a brief digression is necessary. As suggested in the opening chapter, we need to think about number, not as something apart from or opposed to the word, but as a necessary component of language. In this view, a number *is* a word, although a special class of word, and the question then arises: What kind of word is a number? We know that number exists in ordinary language to express measure and quantity. It furnishes a precise account of what is countable; it allows us to calculate and to predict by means of calculation. Hence, by convention, number words in a language signify inflexible absolute values, and this constancy, this invariance, is crucial—if purely axiomatic.[11] The *concrete* nature of number is not only a practical necessity of accounting but the firm ground on which abstract systems may be built. In contrast to the rigidity of number, one ranges the plasticity of words, the ability of a single word to yield up divergent, even antithetical meanings, or different shades of meaning in different contexts; to alter connotations; to denote, over time, a meaning entirely different from the original sense. Add to these kinds of flexibility the ironic or covert uses of words and the ephemera of language, buzzwords and slang expressions that bubble up and disappear; include the idiomatic distortions that affiliate one with a region; and one has an indication of the infinite variability possible to the word. Human expression requires both modes for its various purposes, and language encompasses both.

An author, a poet, a wordsmith is by nature hypersensitive to the workings and shadings and rhythms of language. Morrison illustrates this sensitivity when she explains why she preferred numerals to spelled-out number words for the opening sentences of *Beloved*: "There is something about numerals that makes them spoken, heard, in this context. . . . And the sound of the novel, sometimes cacophonous, sometimes harmonious, must be an inner ear sound or a sound just beyond hearing, infusing the text with a musical emphasis that words can do sometimes even better than music can."[12] The point I want to make also concerns the use of number in a literary context, but it is more general. Most simply, when an author uses number, or a numerical series, or an alphanumerical construct, that author calls into play the most precise indicators, the most abstract entities, the most rigidly inflexible counters, the most coldly objective mode of expression available to language. What could be more opposed to the narrative confusion, or the kaleidoscope of emotion generated in Morrison's novel—hatred, terror, fury, smouldering resentment, horror, pity, frustrated love—and what would be better able to contain them?

These considerations suggest a rationale for the high frequency of number talk in *Beloved*. Among the incidence of numerals and number names, the following items seem to me to be particularly significant: (1) the address at Bluestone Road, (2) the names of the farmhands at "Sweet Home," (3) the oblique reference to the sex act that buys an inscription on a gravestone, (4) Schoolmaster's "scientific" study of his slaves, (5) Paul D's "riff" on that study: "You got two feet, Sethe, not four," and 6) the frequent choice of "sixes" for numerical designations. We can take these in turn.

The place at 124 Bluestone Road "didn't have a number" when Sethe first came to live there, because, we are told, "Cincinnati didn't stretch that far" (2). From a negative point of view, one might say that the numberless house lacked definition as much as the winter landscape and the house itself lacked color. But the numerals 1 2 4 suggest both the establishment of right proportion and the idea of positive increase. On the one hand is the ratio (1 : 2 :: 2 : 4) and on the other the beginning of several possible geometric series, the most obvious (using base 2) a doubling of quantities to infinity (1, 2, 4, 8, 16, 32, 64, 128 . . .). Whether this indicates a welcome fertility or an endless accretion of troubles I cannot tell. It seems evident, however, that the notion of rational relation, of measured proportion suggested by the numerals "1 2 4," is attached to the very same walls that circumscribe activities of the most irrational sort: poltergeist knockings, wailing and breakage, pools of bloodred light. Perhaps the remainder of the address—Bluestone Road—supplies a link between the haunted, bespooked interior and the staid facade. "Bluestone" yields up familiar Morrison motifs: *Bluest one*, and *Blue stone*, like stony "bluest eyes." Or to split it another way, it suggests the *Blues tone*, or simply "the blues." But *bluestone* also means copper sulfate, or *blue vitriol*, familiarly known as "sulfuric acid." In the figurative sense, to "pour vitriol" means to savagely denigrate. Morrison tells us that "the subliminal, the underground life of a novel," is the dimension that facilitates identification. Surely, "Bluestone Road" sends a subliminal message from the start: here is the locus of depression, the resort of stony oppression, a site with a caustic, biting, savage atmosphere. Which brings us to the farmhands under Schoolteacher at Sweet Home, and to their alphanumerical designations.

Six men originally "belonged" to the Sweet Home farm, although one had been sold by the widowed Mrs. Garner, we are told, to pay off debts. As much as any other single element, their names suggest stock in trade: Paul D Garner, Paul F Garner, Paul A Garner, Halle Suggs, and Sixo, "the wild man." The name "Paul" attaches to Morrison's epigraph taken from Rom. 9:25—Saint Paul preaching to the gentiles, having wandered far from home: "I will call them my people, which were not my people; and her beloved, which was not beloved." But the repeated use of "Paul" for the farmhands makes the name an icon of identicality, not a marker of identity, while the Garner "family name" merely underscores the fact of ownership. Letter designations are abruptly replaced with number when we get to "Sixo." We learn that Sixo has had an epic relationship with Patsy, a young girl they all know as his "Thirty-Mile Woman"—the "friend of my mind" he calls her; she, Isis-like, puts the pieces together when he feels torn apart. "She gather me, man. The pieces I am, she gather them and give them back to me in all the right order" (272–73).[13] One doesn't care to stretch the numerology too far, but six followed by zero is sixty, which suggests the idea of thirty-mile Patsy as his "better half." The more delicate irony is Sixo's reversal of the dehumanizing number name into a clarion call of triumph. Just before Sixo, tied to a tree, is shot to death, his final victory is encoded in the shout of *Seven-O! Seven-O!* "because his Thirty-Mile Woman got away with his blossoming seed" (228–29). His "line" is carried forward in the unborn child Patsy carries, and the child is "owned"—that is, spiritually legitimized—by the naming of the father.

SEX, DEATH, AND SIXES

The poetics of naming are intrinsic to the primal scene that gathers into itself every elemental passion, every abuse of person, every corruption of power, every perversion of grace in the work. The nerve center of Morrison's *Beloved* is the love-death scene at the graveyard. And, as Morrison makes clear, "love" refers to the murdered child, not to the sexual act performed—or endured—as payment for its name on the stone. It's not "for free" as the engraver says. Sethe's anguish, humiliation, and dedication are encoded in a five-word "equation" that coolly balances a quantity of time against a quantity of letters and a baby's identity.

"Ten minutes for seven letters." This is the cost of a name—*BELOVED*—chiseled on a headstone "pink as a fingernail . . . and sprinkled with glittering chips." The ten minutes is lived over and over for Sethe:

"Rutting among the stones under the eyes of the engraver's son was not enough. Not only did she have to live out her years in a house palsied by the baby's fury at having its throat cut, but those ten minutes she spent pressed up against dawn-colored stone studded with star chips, her knees wide open as the grave, were longer than life, more alive, more pulsating than the baby blood that soaked her fingers like oil" (5). It's not for free. Sethe exchanges the only saleable good she has to pay for the name chiseled in granite. The costly ten minutes buys the one thing her soul craves: a lasting memorial, a *written* record.

Karla Holloway has pointed out, in "*Beloved:* A Spiritual," the historical thrust of this need for a written record. "Slavery itself defies traditional historiography. The victim's own chronicles of these events were systematically submerged . . . by 'historians' of the [post-emancipation] era."[14] In Holloway's view, Morrison's *Beloved* construes "the consequences of black invisibility in both the records of slavery and the record-keeping as a situation of primary spiritual significance," and this unfulfilled need explains the "ghostly/historical presence that intrudes itself" into the novel, embodied in the character of "Beloved." As I believe, the same desire for a written record elevates the sexual act among the headstones from ten minutes of physical depravity to a declaration of spiritual warfare. Morrison compresses this charged material into the chilling entry that effaces everything but the bare particles of language (numbers, letters): *Ten minutes for seven letters.* We can almost see "schoolteacher" timing the performance.

Schoolteacher is the archenemy of the piece. If at one level Sethe personifies "seething" hot rage, then Schoolteacher is cold calculation, quantification's champion. On the one hand, he calls up Zora Neale Hurston's "schoolteacher" who rapes Janie Crawford's mother—and wrecks her life. On the other, Morrison's compulsive quantifier recalls Dickens's harsh schoolmaster in *Hard Times*: "Thomas Gradgrind, sir. A man of realities. A man of facts and calculations. A man who proceeds upon the principle that two and two are four, and nothing over. . . . Thomas Gradgrind, sir. . . . With a rule and a pair of scales, and the multiplication table always in his pocket, sir, ready to weigh and measure any parcel of human nature, and tell you exactly what it comes to."[15] Gradgrind's students are numbered, of course, not named—"Girl number twenty unable to define a horse!"—and his "scientific" mode of equine definition memorable.

In *Beloved*, Sethe remembers the measuring string and counting of teeth: "Schoolteacher'd wrap that string all over my head, 'cross my nose, around my behind. Number my teeth" (191). In *Hard Times*, the celebrated "definition" of a horse consists largely of a numbering of teeth: "Quadruped. Graminivorous. Forty teeth, namely twenty-four grinder, four eye-teeth, and twelve incisive. . . . Age known by marks in mouth."[16] Sethe's moment of intellectual humiliation occurs when she finds *herself* being defined as two stark rows of facts. "No, no," she overhears Schoolteacher correcting his nephews, "I told you to put her human characteristics on the left; her animal ones on the right. And don't forget to line them up" (193). Even more strikingly Dickensian, however, is Morrison's connection of her own fact-bound Schoolteacher with the motif of the horse. Schoolteacher's equivalence of horse-animal and slave-animal is particularly plain, in Morrison's text, at the scene of the bloodletting.

The infanticide is set at the novel's center, and in case there might be any doubt, Morrison spells out *Apocalypse* for us by launching the chapter with four pale riders: "When the four horsemen came—schoolteacher, one nephew, one slavecatcher and a sheriff—the house on Bluestone Road was so quiet they thought they were too late" (148). Taking in two little boys bleeding in the sawdust and observing Sethe, who holds a blood-soaked child to her chest with one hand and an infant by the heels in the other, Schoolteacher regrets "the mishandling of the nephew who'd overbeat her and made her cut and run." The narrator observes: "Schoolteacher had chastised that nephew, telling him to think—just think—what would his own horse do if you beat it beyond the point of education" (149).

Refutation of the horse/slave equation is reserved for Paul D, who is driven to remind Sethe that she is *not* an animal. We know that on leaving Sweet Farm, Paul D almost literally is turned into a draught horse. As a horse may tremble at a stranger's touch, Paul D's terrible trembling begins when, with a bit in his mouth and driven by a stranger, he turns his head to have a last look at a favorite tree, turning "as much as the rope that connected his neck to the axle of a buckboard allowed" (106). His own experience lends force to the words he uses to confront Sethe when he learns of the infanticide: "You got two feet, Sethe, not four."

His own inarticulable experience in the Georgia prison is strewn with number. In the two passages of verbatim quotation that follow, the most notable dialectical element is the high frequency of number words (appearing in italics). They seem to buttress, or to channel, or to encase, the particulars of the experience they help to describe, as well as lending them a certain monstrous precision. The first passage follows Paul D's capture after attempting to escape his new owner:

[W]hen they fastened the iron around his ankles and clamped the wrists as well, there was no outward sign of trembling at all. Nor *eighteen days* after that when he saw the ditches; the *one thousand feet* of earth—*five feet* deep, *five feet* wide, into which wooden boxes had been fitted. A door of bars that you could lift on hinges like a cage opened into *three walls* and a roof of scrap lumber and red dirt. *Two feet* of it over his head; *three feet* of open trench in front of him with anything that crawled or scurried welcome to share that grave calling itself quarters. And there were *forty-five* more. He was sent there after trying to kill Brandywine, the man schoolteacher sold him to. Brandywine was leading him in a coffle with *ten* others, through Kentucky into Virginia. (106)

The second passage recounts morning "discipline" at the prison camp:

All *forty-six* men woke to rifle shot. All *forty-six*. *Three* whitemen walked along the trench unlocking the doors *one by one*. *No one* stepped through. When the last lock was opened, the *three* returned and lifted the bars, *one by one*. And *one by one* the blackmen emerged—promptly and without the poke of a rifle butt if they had been there more than *a day*; promptly with the butt if, like Paul D, they had just arrived. When *all forty-six* were standing in a line in the trench, another rifle shot signaled the climb out and up to the ground above, where *one thousand feet* of the best hand-forged iron chain in Georgia stretched.... Chain up completed, they knelt down.... Kneeling in the mist they waited for the whim of *a guard*, or *two*, or *three*. Or maybe *all* of them wanted it. Wanted it from *one* prisoner in particular or *none*—or *all*. (107)

Immediately between these passages, held together by them, so to speak, is a graphic physical account of Paul D's uncontrollable trembling that contains but one reference to number: a reference to a time span of "twenty years." Similarly, the brief dialogue and the narrative that follows the second number-laden passage describes sexual and psychological obscenities visited upon the prisoners, and contains no number words. But this scene of sexual humiliation (paralleling Sethe's "ten minutes") is initiated at the point where elementary numbers are replaced by abstractions—*all*, and *none* or *all*—as shown above. I believe that it is Morrison's almost choreographic deployment of number and cool abstraction, in the development of these episodes, that leads the reader into the purest experience of atrocity.

Beyond Lamentation

In the much-quoted final sentence of the *Tractatus*, the singular Proposition 7, Wittgenstein remarks on the inexpressible realm of human experience that exists outside the universe of logic: "Whereof one cannot speak, thereof one must be silent" [*Wovon man nicht sprechen kann, darüber muss man schweigen*]. One commentator on the *Tractatus* notes that "some of the most important remarks in the text are a number of what might be called 'principles of linguistic impotence,' statements about what *cannot* be expressed in language."[17] While "what cannot be spoken" (*Unaussprechliches*) refers in this case to mystical experience, Wittgenstein's proposition of ultimate inexpressibility applies equally to suffering and pain, and a later work in fact takes up the unknowability of another's pain.[18] Morrison, pursuing a logic of her own, attempts to *record* "unspeakable thoughts, unspoken" (199), that is, to set down in hard print subject matter that has not been admitted into frontal consciousness, or social conscience. In fact, the whole thrust of Morrison's *Beloved* is to show the reverse face of the coin: "Whereof one cannot remain silent, thereof one must speak." But extraordinary suffering cannot be articulated by words used for ordinary experience. Here the notion of "linguistic impotence" holds firm. As we have seen, however, one can suggest such experience through calculated understatement, oblique reference, and indirection, or one can enclose the naked account of atrocity in devices of number and measure. These quantitative structures, empty of all but rational indices, have the ability—and this, I think, is what is so striking—to support implications of a qualitative nature. Morrison so deploys them, strategically and effectively, to move us somewhere beyond lamentation. In this ghostly and historic novel, Morrison uses one specific number—six—as an unmoved mover.

In the context of unspeakable human suffering, the concentration of sixes in *Beloved* has particular force. Not only are the eighteen years that constitute its time span a factor of six, but we find that there were six slaves who belonged to Sweet Home, that Baby Suggs had six husbands, that Sethe was married to Halle for six years, that she escaped in her sixth month of pregnancy, and bore a "6-month baby." The indigo slave with tongue of flame (21) who triumphs both physically and spiritually at the scene of his destruction is named *Sixo*. But it is Morrison's dedication of the novel to "Sixty Million / and more" that links a people's experience of profound suffering, not only to the uncountable victims of the Middle Passage, the barracoons, and the plantations, but to the six million exterminated in Nazi death camps. Six in all: Auschwitz, Treblinka, Sobibor, Majdenek, Belsen, Buchenwald. Neither the Sixty Million nor the Six Million are actual counts; they are "tactful" representative numbers that point in the general direction of a genocide one cannot really talk about.

The number six, of course, is not the sole link with Hebrew experience in Morrison's novel. The title itself calls up the Shulamite, the spouse in the Old Testament's *Song of Solomon*—the betrothed who chants "I am black but comely." In Solomon's love poem, we hear: "I am my beloved's, and my beloved is mine" (6:3), and "I am my beloved's, and his desire is toward me" (7:10). The refrain of the Shulamite is echoed in the opening lines of chapters 2, 4, and 5 of part 2 in Morrison's novel. Sethe says: "Beloved, she my daughter. She mine," affirming the identity of the child and the legitimacy of the family tie, as Sixo has done. And Beloved responds to the mother twice, liturgically: "I am Beloved and she is mine" ("she" meaning Sethe). In "Toni Morrison's Ghost: The Beloved Who Is Not Beloved," Elizabeth House points out, accurately I think, that "chapters four and five of Part II must be read as a poem . . . examining the text line by line."[19] In *Beloved*, the hollow echo of the biblical love song ("I love him because he has a song") twists into a grotesque elegiac meditation on death and the loss of the lover—notably devoid of punctuation:

> the others do not know he is dead   I know   his song is gone
>   now I love his pretty little teeth instead
>
> (211–12)

The syntactic fragmentation, the blank holes between word clusters, is symbolic and strikingly graphic; Morrison is using the page as the unit of space as a poet might.

Perhaps the most deeply telling linkage of black history with Hebrew history is at the heart of the novel in the unthinkable act of infanticide. This is not the mythic act of a mythic Medea, made tragically desperate by a husband's abandonment.[20] Nor is it the trashing of unwanted infants we hear reported on the ten o'clock news. As Holloway, Bell, and others have noted, and as Morrison herself has pointed out, the infanticide *and* its time frame are drawn from American history—

the murder of her child by Margaret Garner, a slave, who refused to yield up her baby to the slave owners.[21] Bernard Bell succinctly recapitulates "Morrison's retelling of the chilling historical account of a compassionate yet resolute self-emancipated mother's tough love. Margaret Garner, with the tacit sympathy of her sexagenarian mother-in-law, cut the throat of one of her four children and tried to kill the others to save them from the outrages of slavery that she had suffered."[22] Holloway adds the information that "Morrison refused to do any further research on Margaret Garner beyond her reviewing of the magazine article that recounted the astonishment of the preacher and journalists who found her to be 'very calm . . . very serene' after murdering her child."[23] In *Beloved*, following the usage of the slave owners, the family name of "Garner" is extended both to the Sweet Home owners and their slaves. But in Morrison's novel, this "gathering together" under one family name implicates the slave owners in the murder.

To kill one's own child in order to forestall something far worse points to soul struggle of an intensity that, quite possibly, has no parallel. I should like to suggest that, added to joint experiences of exile, exclusion, and extermination, the story of Margaret Garner forges still another, more personal, historic link between two peoples. One does not know if Morrison herself was aware of such a linkage, but that there *is* a written account to consult preserves a certain distinction. We find the record in Durant, in the bare facts of an eleventh-century pogrom during the First Crusade. Durant's account calls up scenes and actions that resonate in *Beloved*—the hunting down and killing of innocent people, and the sacrifice of beloved infants:

> Arrived at Speyer [moving south along the Rhine], the Crusaders dragged eleven Jews into a church, and ordered them to accept baptism; refusing, the eleven were slain [3 May 1096]. . . . As some Crusaders neared Trier, its Jews appealed to Bishop Egilbert; he offered protection on condition of baptism. Most of the Jews consented; but *several women killed their children and threw themselves into the Moselle* [1 June 1096). At Mainz Archbishop Ruthard hid 1300 Jews in his cellars; Crusaders forced their way in, and killed 1,014. . . . As the Crusaders approached Cologne . . . the mob burned down the Jewish quarter, and killed the few Jews upon whom they could lay their hands. . . . [The pilgrims] hunted their prey in the villages, and killed every Jew they found [June 1096]. In two . . . villages 200 Jews were slain; in four others the Jews, surrounded by the mob, killed one another rather than be baptized. *Mothers delivered of infants during these attacks slew them at birth.*[24]

In a 1991 essay, "Black Matter(s)," Toni Morrison talks of the trope of blackness and the "typology of diabolism" in storytelling (romance, the Gothic) as a method by which one group of people projects its worst fears onto the ethnic Other; she invites her reader to consider the "effect of racialism on those who perpetuate it."[25] In matters of race, she contends, "silence and evasion have historically ruled literary discourse." While every one of Morrison's works runs counter to silence and evasion on the sociopolitical level, it is *Beloved* that most nearly conveys the inexpressible. It is the genius of *Beloved* to generalize from a black woman named Sethe to the pain of Afro-America, its men as well as its women. It is the genius of *Beloved* to generalize beyond color, beyond the black experience alone, to racial suffering and the diabolical typology that continues, as energetically as it always has, to twist the knife in the wound. Against linguistic impotence Morrison has ranged the beloved word, armed all around with number, to force some acknowledgment of the unspeakable facts.

Notes

CHAPTER 1. THE TELLTALE FIGURE

1. Cited in Betsy Devine, *An Abelian Grape: and Other Off-Color Jokes of Mathematical Flavor*, limited ed. (Princeton, N.J.: privately published, 1990), 20–21. The material in this edition was expanded in a later volume by the same author: *Absolute Zero Gravity: A Collection of Jokes, Anecdotes, Limericks, and Riddles, Revealing the Funny Side of Physics, Biology, Mathematics, and Other Branches of Science* (New York: Simon & Schuster, 1992).

2. William Carlos Williams, "The Great Figure," in *The Collected Poems of William Carlos Williams*, vol. 1: *1909–1939*, ed. A. Walton Litz and Christopher MacGowan (New York: New Directions, 1986), 174. Bram Dijkstra, in *The Hieroglyphics of a New Speech: Cubism, Stieglitz, and the Early Poetry of William Carlos Williams* (Princeton: Princeton University Press, 1969) reads the poem as an image that "flashes" onto the poet's field of awareness—a montage of visual tensions—and quotes Dr. Williams' *Autobiography* as to the genesis of the poem: "Once on a hot July day coming back exhausted from the Post Graduate Clinic, I dropped in as I sometimes did at Marsden's studio on Fifteenth Street for a talk, a little drink maybe and to see what he was doing. As I approached his number I heard a great clatter of bells and the roar of a fire engine passing the end of the street down Ninth Avenue. I turned just in time to see a golden figure 5 on a red background flash by. The impression was so sudden and forceful that I took a piece of paper out of my pocket and wrote a short poem about it" (Dijkstra, *Hieroglyphics*, 76).

3. Aristotle, *De motu animalium* 1.698^{a}25, trans. A. S. L. Farquharson, in vol. 5 of *The Complete Works of Aristotle*, ed. J. A. Smith and W. D. Ross (Oxford: Clarendon, 1912). The philosopher is here contrasting the "centres" of animal motion (joints) and the indivisible "centre" of geometric illustration.

4. Morris Klein, *Mathematical Thought from Ancient to Modern Times* (New York: Oxford University Press, 1972), 132. Sir Thomas Heath notes, in *A History of Greek Mathematics*, vol. 1 (New York: Oxford University Press, 1921),

that there have been two views on the use of the alphabet symbols for calculation (38) and quotes James Gow, in *A Short History of Greek Mathematics* (reprint, New York: Hafner, 1923): "[T]he alphabetic numerals were a fatal mistake and hopelessly confined such nascent arithmetical faculty as the Greeks may have possessed" (46).

5. Karl Menninger, *Number Words and Number Symbols: A Cultural History of Numbers*, trans. Paul Broneer (Cambridge: MIT Press, 1969), 45.

6. Studies of mystical numerology are plentiful, often going back to Pythagorean proportions and number relations, Plato's *Timaeus*, or the *Zohar*. Useful works on Pythagorean symbolism and proportion are Rudolf Wittkower, *Architectural Principles in the Age of Humanism*, 4th ed. (London and New York: St. Martin's Press, 1988); Christopher Butler, *Number Symbolism* (London: Routledge & Kegan Paul, 1970); and Annemarie Schimmel, *The Mystery of Numbers* (Oxford: Oxford University Press, 1993). A widely used reference is Vincent Foster Hopper, *Medieval Number Symbolism: Its Sources, Meaning, and Influence on Thought and Expression* (New York: Columbia University Press, 1938). Frances A. Yates's *Giordano Bruno and the Hermetic Tradition* (Chicago: University of Chicago Press, 1964) remains a model of lucidity in discussing the most enigmatic of subjects. An excellent entry into Hebrew mystical practices can be found in Gershom Scholem, *Major Trends in Jewish Mysticism*, 3d rev. ed. (New York: Schocken Books, 1954), and idem, *Jewish Mysticism in the Middle Ages* (New York: Judaica Press, 1964). More recently, Paul Oppenheimer's *The Birth of the Modern Mind: Self-Consciousness and the Invention of the Sonnet* (New York: Oxford University Press, 1989) provides a concise, clear, and particularly useful discussion of Pythagorean harmonic proportion, in Plato's *Timaeus*, as it affects the formal development of the sonnet and reflects an ordered yet flexible modality of thinking.

7. Such words, present in many archaic languages according to the nineteenth-century philologist, Karl Abel, exerted an ongoing fascination on Freud. See Sigmund Freud, "The Antithetical Meanings of Primal Words" (1910), in *The Standard Edition of the Complete Psychological Works of Sigmund Freud*, trans. James Strachey (London: Hogarth Press, 1955), 2:155–61. Also see 13:67; 15:79; 15:229-30, 23:169.

8. See M. M. Bakhtin, *The Dialogic Imagination: Four Essays*, trans. Michael Holquist and Caryl Emerson (Austin: University of Texas Press, 1981). I have singled out Bakhtin in this context, rather than Saussure or Heidegger or Derrida or de Man, because Bakhtin has contributed greatly to the understanding of the multidimensionality of language, and thus to a realization of what language is capable of conveying. In contrast, one has the emphasis on absence, the impossibility of determining meaning, the negational focus that constitutes the main arena of *langue/parole* linguistic models, or Heideggerian phenomenological notions of language, or the "aporias" and "undoings" and "effacements" of deconstructive theory. While interesting in themselves as powerful models of the *negativa*, they do not help to distinguish the character of the word as opposed to the character of number. In fact, one might contend that the inevitable loss of meaning between signifier and signified, in contemporary

theory, approximates most closely a mathematical construct of infinite regression.

9. Gilberto Perez, "The Narrative Sequence," *Hudson Review* 30, no. 1 (spring 1977): 80–92.

10. Ibid., 80.

11. Erich Auerbach, "Figura," in *Scenes from the Drama of European Literature,* trans. Ralph Manheim (Gloucester, Mass.: Peter Smith, 1973), 15. Auerbach's invaluable study develops the changing values of the term from its Latin beginnings in Plautus, Lucretius, Ovid, and Quintilian, through "typological" uses in the church fathers—from Tertullian to Augustine to Aquinas—and concludes with Dante's historical/allegorical figure of Beatrice in the *Vita Nuova* and the visionary figure of the great Rose of the *Paradiso.*

12. The later Wittgenstein's model of "family resemblance" is quickly illustrated by his discussion, in *The Brown Book,* of the proposition: "There is a family of friendly facial expressions." See Ludwig Wittgenstein, *The Blue and Brown Books: Preliminary Studies for the "Philosophical Investigations,"* 2d rev. ed. (New York: Harper, 1960), 145. I am indebted to Angus Fletcher for bringing this proposition to my attention.

13. For an invaluable study of letter play in Wallace Stevens's poetry, see Philip Furia and Martin Roth, "Stevens' Fusky Alphabet," *PMLA* 93, no. 1 (January 1978): 66–77. The authors quote Stevens's assertion that "A" is "an infant . . . standing on infant legs" and that "Z" is a "twisted, stooping" old man "that kneels always on the edge of space" (66), while Stevens's logico-mathematical use of letters to introduce premises is illustrated by Furia and Roth in the late poem, "The Rock":

> The rock is the habitation of the whole,
> Its strength and measure, that which is near,
>   point A
> In a perspective that begins again
>
> At B.

(69)

14. For reference to the "O-groan" in the context of Elizabethan drama, see chap. 2, note 8.

15. Among the romantic poets, the "I" of identity and of lonely singleness may be found in conjunction with the spherical emblems of sun and moon in Samuel Taylor Coleridge's *The Rime of the Ancient Mariner* (1798), part II; while the symbolic albatross in this poem suggests a remarkable conjoining of primary letter *and* number symbols: A (AL-) and B (BA-) and TROSS (the "TR-" for three) in its trinity of syllables.

16. Fermat's Last Theorem developed from his method of infinite descent (noted in chap. 3), which he used to prove that there is no cube that is divisible into two cubes—that is, that there are no positive integers x, y, and z such that $x^3 + y^3 = z^3$. His general proposition—the famous Last Theorem—stated that

for an n integer greater than two, there are no positive integral values x, y, and z such that $x^n + y^n = z^n$. He wrote in the margin of his copy of Bachet's *Diophantes* that he had a "truly marvelous" proof of this theorem "which this margin is too narrow to contain." See Carl B. Boyer, *A History of Mathematics* (Princeton: Princeton University Press, 1985), 387–88.

In 1993, Andrew Wiles of Princeton University announced during the third of a series of lectures delivered at Cambridge University that he had solved the problem using the Shimura-Taniyama-Weil conjecture developed in the study of elliptic curves (the connection first being found in 1984 by Gerhard Frey). The claim has since been withdrawn, although, at this writing, Wiles's solution has been reaffirmed and newly reestablished, and the Last Theorem appears finally to be solved. I am grateful to Benji Fisher of Columbia University for this information, as well as for monitoring various mathematical concepts treated in this study.

17. G. S. Kirk and J. E. Raven, *The Presocratic Philosophers* (Cambridge: Cambridge University Press, 1963), 227. At this writing, the most comprehensive coverage of the cluster of terms designating the state or act or process or relationship deriving from the root term that has the basic meaning "to direct one's mind to something"—*manthǎno, katamanthǎno, mathetés, summathetés, mathétria, matheteúo*—may be found in the *Theological Dictionary of the New Testament*, ed. Gerhard Kittel (Grand Rapids, Mich.: Wm. B. Eerdman's, 1942–67), 4:390ff. I am grateful to my colleague in classics, Marshall Hurwitz, for pointing me to this source and for his invaluable help in many aspects of this study.

18. See Jason L. Saunders, *Greek and Roman Philosophy after Aristotle* (New York: The Free Press, 1966). Chap. 3, "Skepticism," contains a translation of Sextus Empiricus's "Outlines of Pyrrhonism" (152–82). I am indebted to the late Professor Saunders for the alternate translation of *Kata mathematikoi* as *Against the Grammarians*.

19. Benjamin Banneker (1731–1806), by occupation a farmer, was taught to read by his grandmother and attended a Quaker's school. He pursued his chief interest in mathematics, and eventually became known as mathematician, naturalist, astronomer, inventor, poet, and compiler of almanacs. For further information, see Shirley Grahams' biography, *Your Most Humble Servant* (1949), and Henry E. Baker's scholarly article, "Benjamin Banneker, The Negro Mathematician and Astronomer," *Journal of Negro History* 3 (1918): 99–118. I am grateful to my colleague, Professor James de Jongh, for bringing Banneker's mathematical problems in verse to my attention.

20. See Scott Buchanan, *Poetry and Mathematics* (New York: John Day, 1929). The author (b. 1895) taught high-school Greek and mathematics while an undergraduate at Amherst College, studied philosophy at Oxford as a Rhodes Scholar, and taught philosophy at Harvard, The City College of New York, and the University of Virginia. The seven chapters that follow the introductory chapter, "Poetry and Mathematics," take up "Figures," "Numbers," "Proportions," "Equations," "Functions," "Symbols," and "Tragedy and Comedy." For English majors, and other students of the "soft" disciplines, Buchanan holds out hope:

Mathematics suffers much, but most of all from its teachers. As a result of bad pedagogy . . . the appearance of an algebraic formula, a geometrical figure, or an innocent set of symbols reduces the reader to an unbecoming attitude of hypocritical humility. [These students] persuade themselves they haven't mathematical minds, when as a matter of fact they have only had non-mathematical teachers. Mathematics is not what most teachers of mathematics teach. (5)

21. Ludwig Wittgenstein, *Philosophical Grammar*, trans. Anthony Kenny (Berkeley and Los Angeles: University of California Press, 1974), 381-82. The reference to the Goldbach Conjecture ("theorem") as part of an extended meditation on the nature of mathematical propositions occurs on p. 381.

22. For accounts of Wittgenstein's life, interests, and personal characteristics, see Rush Rhees, ed. *Ludwig Wittgenstein: Personal Recollections* (Totowa, N.J.: Rowman & Littlefield, 1981), of which the memoir by F. R. Leavis seems to me of particular interest (63–80); the architect Paul Engelmann's *Letters from Ludwig Wittgenstein: with a Memoir* (New York: Horizon Press, 1968), is a sympathetic memoir that contains LW's note to a prospective publisher of the *Tractatus* stating that the "book's point is an ethical one" and that "it draws limits to the sphere of the ethical from the inside as it were" (143–44). William Warren Bartley takes up the question of Wittgenstein's sexuality in *Wittgenstein*, 2d rev. ed. (LaSalle, Ill.: Open Court,1985), and helpfully covers in detail the years Wittgenstein taught in Trattenbach, in southern Austria. The definitive literary biography, to date, is Ray Monk's *Ludwig Wittgenstein: The Duty of Genius* (New York: The Free Press, 1990); it includes a fine selection of photographs and a comprehensive coverage of LW's philosophy and mathematics, as well as a detailed life. Extremely useful, for general context, intellectual influences, and a sense of the elusive *Zeitgeist*, is Allan Janik and Stephen Toulmin, *Wittgenstein's Vienna* (New York: Simon & Schuster, 1973).

23. On Wittgenstein's Cartesian metaphor of "logical space," philosopher Max Black comments: "Objects are like the co-ordinates of empty positions in physical space, atomic facts are like the material points that sometimes occupy such positions. . . . talk about 'logical space' proves to be a picturesque way of talking about the relations between objects and atomic facts." See Max Black, *A Companion to Wittgenstein's "Tractatus"* (Ithaca: Cornell University Press, 1964), 9–10.

24. See Ludwig Wittgenstein, *Remarks on the Foundations of Mathematics*, ed. G. H. von Wright, Rush Rhees, and G. E. M. Anscombe, trans. G. E. M. Anscombe, rev. ed. (Cambridge: MIT Press, 1983), 38. LW asks, "How should we get into conflict with truth, if our footrules were made of very soft rubber instead of wood and steel?" After a short discussion he proposes: "If a [soft rubber] ruler expanded to an extraordinary extent when slightly heated, we should say—in normal circumstances—that made it *unusable*. But we could think of a situation in which this was just what was wanted. I am imagining that we perceive the expansion with the naked eye; and we ascribe the same numerical measure of length to bodies in rooms of different temperatures,

if they measure the same by the ruler which to the eye is now longer, now shorter."

25. For the "subliming of logic" (*die Sublimierung der ganzen Darstellung*) see Ludwig Wittgenstein, *Philosophical Investigations*, trans. G. E. M. Anscombe (New York: Macmillan, 1953), 44, 44e. For the "inexorability" of mathematical series and rules, see Wittgenstein's *Remarks on the Foundations of Mathematics*, p. 37, §4—"what does the peculiar inexorability of mathematics consist in?"—and p. 318 § 16.

26. See Ludwig Wittgenstein, *Philosophical Investigations*, p. 8e, §19 for "language as a form of life"; and p. 47e, §109 for the "bewitchment" remark.

27. See Ludwig Wittgenstein, *Culture and Value*, trans. Peter Winch (Chicago: University of Chicago Press, 1984), 25e.

28. Juliet H. Floyd, "The Rule of the Mathematical: Wittgenstein's Later Discussions" (Ph.D. diss., Harvard University, 1990), 107. A portion of this thesis has been published as "Wittgenstein on 2, 2, 2 . . . : The Opening of Remarks on the Foundations of Mathematics," *Synthese* 87 (1991): 143–80. This study not only elucidates Wittgenstein's comments with clarity and elegance, but demonstrates the position of the "interlocutor" as both a foil and as a dialogical presenter of perspectives. It has sharpened my understanding both of the mathematical constructs and the philosophical positions in question, and I am most grateful for the chance to read it in unhurried circumstances.

29. Wittgenstein, *Remarks on the Foundations of Mathematics*, p. 38, § 4.

30. Juliet Floyd, "The Rule of the Mathematical," 118.

31. Although the chapters ahead do not take up the legends of the *Táin Bo Culainn*, the Cuchulainn tales, or Goethe's eighteenth-century best-seller, *The Sorrows of Young Werther*, both contain notable mathematical structuring. Books 9 and 10 of *The Táin* are structured by number and color to a remarkable extent, and book 9 in particular uses repetitions of each number in a passage that intensifies the use of the series of natural numbers. Goethe uses "clocking," the measured passage of time, to heighten the tension of the hours leading to his hero's love-suicide. Perhaps more noteworthy, in this context, is the "silhouette" of Lotte's profile—a black mirror image that serves to show her absence in Werther's life—a geometric figure of negation.

32. Wittgenstein, *Remarks on the Foundations of Mathematics*, p. 99, § 168.

33. Ludwig Wittgenstein, *Culture and Value*, 84e.

CHAPTER 2: ZERO REASON, INFINITE NEED

1. William Blake, "The Marriage of Heaven and Hell," plate 4, in *The Poetry and Prose of William Blake*, ed. David V. Erdman and Harold Bloom (New York: Doubleday, 1965).

2. William Elton points out that Regan and Goneril respect material wealth and physical strength. Their "contempt for their father," he adds, "is partly involved with their criterion of natural potency." See *King Lear and the Gods* (San Marino, Calif.: Huntington Library, 1968), 121.

3. *King Lear*, ed. Kenneth Muir, The Arden Edition of the Works of William Shakespeare (London and New York: Methuen, 1972). All line numbers placed in parentheses following citation of text refer to this edition.

4. The colon is to syntax what the equals sign is to an equation: both signal that equivalent values occur on each side of the symbol. One should note that variations in spelling and punctuation occur here as elsewhere in the plays, a major concern of textual scholarship. Variants in the folios and quartos show the "O" spelled "Oh" and the colon replacing a comma. According to Vietor, the colon (suggestive of a mathematical ratio) that appears in the Folio of 1623 is not present in the earlier 1608 Quarto. See Wilhelm Vietor, *"King Lear": Parallel Texts of the First Quarto and the First Folio* (Marburg, 1892), 70-71. More recently, variations in the texts of the play have been given careful scholarly attention. See William Shakespeare, *The Parallel King Lear, 1608–1623*, prepared by Michael Warren (Berkeley: University of California Press, 1989); *The Division of the Kingdoms: Shakespeare's Two Versions of King Lear*, ed. Gary Taylor and Michael Warren, Oxford Shakespeare Studies (Oxford: Clarendon; New York: Oxford University Press, 1983); and in Steven Urkowitz, *Shakespeare's Revision of "King Lear"* (Princeton: Princeton University Press, 1980).

5. Elton, *King Lear and the Gods*, 329.

6. Angus Fletcher, "The Black Swan and the Bewitching Bedfellow: On *Othello* and the Criticism of its Author" (paper delivered at the Shakespeare Symposium, GSUC-CUNY, April 1981), 14.

7. Ibid., 16.

8. See Maurice Charney, "Hamlet's O-Groans and Textual Criticism," *Renaissance Drama*, n.s., 9 (1978): 109–19.

9. Ibid., 118–19.

10. In this context, I should like to draw attention to William Empson's discussion of the word "all" in *Paradise Lost*, in *The Structure of Complex Words* (Ann Arbor: University of Michigan Press, 1967), 101–4. The same volume also contains Empson's notable chapter, "Fool in Lear" (see 125–57).

11. For an illuminating discussion of the world-upside-down topos in the play, see Joseph Wittreich's *"Image of that Horror": History, Prophecy, and Apocalypse in "King Lear"* (San Marino, Calif.: Huntington Library, 1984), 68–74.

12. Charney remarks ("Hamlet's Groans," p. 111) of this scene, "King Lear's O-groans in the Pied Bull Quarto of 1608 have . . . vanished from modern editions, although in context they have a brute force very apt for the old king's final burst of energy before he dies: 'O thou wilt come no more, neuer, neuer, neuer, pray you vndo this button, thanke you sir, O o o o'" (*King Lear* 5.3.307–8). Quarto 2 (1619) has a string of five "O's" here, whereas the Folio text has five "nevers" and no "O's."

13. It seems likely that the "prop" map would have been inscribed upon a scroll. The scroll may well have contained a round *Mapa Mundi*, or it may have been fashioned on the design of the medieval "T-in-O" map—a circular world *already divided into three sections*. For a discussion of the "T-in-O" map, see *Geography and Literature: A Meeting of the Disciplines*, ed. William E. Mallory and Paul Simson-Housley (Syracuse, N.Y.: Syracuse University Press, 1987), 149,

165–67. I am indebted to my colleague, the late Professor Thomas King, and to Professors Saul Brody and Steven Urkowitz, for their valuable conjectures and suggestions on this point.

14. Empson, "Fool in Lear," 152.

15. Brian Rotman, *Signifying Nothing: The Semiotics of Zero* (New York: St. Martin's Press, 1987), 78. On Robert Recorde's text, also see Boyer, *History of Mathematics*, 317ff. On p. 319, Boyer shows a facsimile page of Robert Recorde's *The Whetstone of Witte* (1557), displaying a number of the arithmetic symbols— such as parallel lines to indicate equivalence, i.e., a long "equals sign"—in use in Shakespeare's sixteenth-century England. Another excellent source of information is Karl Menninger's *Number Words and Number Symbols: A Cultural History of Numbers*, trans. Paul Broneer (Cambridge: MIT Press, 1969). According to Menninger, a "popular and widely read book in [sixteenth-century] England was *The Ground of Arts* of 1541, in which Robert Recorde dealt with arithmetic computations among other topics. Another well-known English book was the St. Albans Book of Computations of 1537: *Introduction for to Lerne to Recken with the Pen or with the Counters*" (337).

16. Rotman, *Signifying Nothing*, 5.

17. Ibid., 83.

18. For information on the entrance of the algorist zero into western mathematics, consult the following excellent histories: Boyer, *A History of Mathematics*, 278–80); Menninger, *Number Words and Number Symbols*, 294ff.; Morris Kline, *Mathematical Thought from Ancient to Modern Times* (New York: Oxford University Press, 1972), esp. 184–85; Howard Eves, *Great Moments in Mathematics (Before 1650)*, Dolciani Mathematical Expositions (Washington, D.C.: Mathematical Assn. of America, c. 1983), esp. 5:160–62, 192–93; Edna E. Kramer, *The Main Stream of Mathematics* (New York: Oxford University Press, 1951), esp. 31–33.

David Eugene Smith, coauthor of *The Hindu-Arabic Numerals* (Boston: Ginn & Co., 1911), discusses the naming of the "zero" in vol. 2 of his *History of Mathematics*: "The name for zero is not settled yet. Modern usage allows it to be called by the name of the letter *O*, an interesting return to the Greek name *omicron* used by Buteo in 1559. The older names are *zero, cipher,* and *naught*. The Hindus called it *sunya,* 'void,' and this term passed over into Arabic as *as-sifr* or *sifr*. When Fibonnaci (1202) wrote his *Liber Abaci*, he spoke of the character as *zephirum* ('quod arabice zephirum appelatur')" (71).

19. Gottlob Frege, *The Foundations of Arithmetic: A Logico-Mathematical Enquiry into the Concept of Number*, trans. J. L. Austin, 2d rev. ed. (Evanston, Ill.: Northwestern University Press, 1980), 115.

20. Ibid., 87, 90.

21. See Jorge Luis Borges, *Labyrinths: Selected Stories and Other Writings* (New York: New Directions, 1964), 189–92. Borges's "Fearful Sphere of Pascal," translated by Anthony Kerrigan and originally published in 1959, preceded by two years Georges Poulet's *The Metamorphoses of the Circle* (Baltimore: Johns Hopkins University Press, 1966), which contained a chapter on Pascal and was published in the French in 1961. Predating both was Marjorie Hope Nicolson's study of the intellectual history of the Circle of Perfection and the evidence for

the decay of that idea in seventeenth-century poetry and thought; see *The Breaking of the Circle: Studies in the Effect of the "New Science" upon Seventeenth-Century Poetry*, rev. ed. (New York: Columbia University Press, 1960). I am indebted to Professor Samuel Mintz for directing me to this fine work. In chapter 47 of Rabelais's *Pantagruel*, the priestess of the oracle sends the travelers on their way with a blessing: "Now, my friends . . . may that intellectual sphere whose centre is everywhere and circumference nowhere, whom we call GOD, keep you in his almighty protection."

Chapter 3. The Mathematics of Pandaemonium

1. Milton's note on "The Verse," set before the Argument of book 1 of *Paradise Lost* (lines 249–50). All page numbers, lineation, and verse citations refer to *The Complete Poetry of John Milton*, ed. John Shawcross, rev. ed. (New York: Anchor Books, 1971).

2. See James Holly Hanford, *John Milton, Englishman* (New York: Crown, 1949), 76–77. Hanford cites Milton's letter in Latin to his friend Bonmattei, written after the poet's visit to Florence, in which he asks who might "claim second place, in Italian letters, to Dante."

3. Also see Harris Francis Fletcher, *Milton's Rabbinical Readings* (New York: Gordian Press, 1967) for a discussion of the *Zohar* in connection with seventeenth-century scholarship (esp. 76, 132). A useful discussion of Milton's connection with the numerology drawn from Plato's *Timaeus* (the prototext for Pythagorean symbolism) may be found in S. K. Henninger's essay, "Sydney and Milton: The Poet as Maker," in *Milton and the Line of Vision*, ed. Joseph Anthony Wittreich Jr. (Madison: University of Wisconsin Press, 1975), 57–95. Also see Christopher Butler, *Number Symbolism* (London: Routledge & Kegan Paul, 1970) and the more recent study by Annemarie Schimmel, *The Mystery of Numbers* (New York and Oxford: Oxford University Press, 1993) for a more general overview of numerology. Alastair Fowler's *Spenser and the Numbers of Time* (Oxford: Routledge & Kegan Paul, 1964) remains the most comprehensive and comprehensible study of Elizabethan numerology.

4. Fowler, *Numbers of Time*, 4.

5. One finds witty parodies on this mode of Euclidean mysticism somewhat later in mid-seventeenth-century lyrics. "The Snayl" from Thomas Traherne's *Lucasta* is a case in point:

> Compendious Snayl! thou seem'st to me,
> Large *Euclids* strikt Epitome;
> And in each Diagram, dost fling
> Thee from the point unto the Ring.
> A Figure now Triangulare,
> An Oval now, and now a Square;
> And then a Serpentine dost crawl
> Now a straight Line, now crook'd, now all.

6. Alastair Fowler, *Triumphal Forms: Structural Patterns in Elizabethan Poetry* (Cambridge: Cambridge University Press, 1970), 119.

7. Paul Oskar Kristeller, "Renaissance Platonism," in *Facets of the Renaissance* (New York: Harper Torchbooks, 1959), 114.

8. The most comprehensive treatment, to date, of Milton's education is the two-volume study by Harris Francis Fletcher, *The Intellectual Development of John Milton* (Champaign: University of Illinois Press, 1956, 1961). Of particular interest here are the chapters on mathematics, and the listings of texts—both in logic and mathematics—in use at the time. For specific information on Milton as tutor, see 1:356ff. A brief but helpful study is William T. Costello, S.J., *The Scholastic Curriculum at Early Seventeenth-Century Cambridge* (Cambridge: Harvard University Press, 1958). The well-known statement of interest in things mathematical I have referred to is in the *Defensio Secunda* (8:120-21), published in 1654.

9. Among the last of Milton's writings was this short treatise on the logic of Peter Ramus (1515–72), a French convert from Roman Catholicism to Protestantism who was murdered during the St. Bartholomew Massacre. His *Dialectica* (1556) set forth an anti-Aristotelian, anti-Scholastic logic, and was a pervasive influence during the sixteenth and seventeenth centuries in France, England, Holland, Belgium, and Scandinavia.

10. Maren Sofie Røstvig, "The Hidden Sense: Milton and the Neoplatonic Method of Numerical Composition," in *The Hidden Sense and Other Essays*, Norwegian Studies in English, 9 (Oslo: Univeritetsforlaget; New York: Humanities Press, 1963), 41.

11. John Milton, *Christian Doctrine*, trans. James Carey, in *Complete Prose Works of John Milton*, ed. Maurice Kelley (New Haven: Yale University Press, 1973), 6:146–47.

12. Ibid., 710-11 (bk. 2, chap. 7).

13. See Auerbach, *Figura*, 11–76. Auerbach defines the concept in general terms as "the creative principle, change amid enduring essence, the shades of meaning between copy and archetype" (49). His study, in the best German philological tradition, covers classical and medieval uses of the term, which, alongside the iconic and rhetorical modes, include appearances also "as idol, as dream figure or vision, as *mathematical form*" (37–38; my emphasis). In an extensive, intelligent discussion of figural elements and epistemological modes in *Paradise Lost*, Linda Gregerson refers to Auerbach's exploration of "figural interpretation" in her fine study of Milton's similes, "The Limbs of Truth: Milton's Use of Simile in *Paradise Lost*," *Milton Studies* 14 (1980): 135–52.

14. Stanley Fish, *Surprised by Sin: The Reader in Paradise Lost* (New York: St. Martin's Press, 1967), 22.

15. The theological resonance of the "rood" or Cross should not be overlooked in this context. Satan lies horizontal on the Flood, a perpendicular inversion of the Crucifixion, while "rood-tree" suggests pain.

16. See James Whaler, "The Miltonic Simile," *PMLA* 46 (1931): 1064, cited in Fish, *Surprised by Sin*, 27.

17. Fish, *Surprised by Sin*, 27.

18. Gregerson, "Limbs of Truth," 140-41 n. 12.

19. For a concise account of this journey, see Douglas Bush, *John Milton: A Sketch of his Life and Writings* (New York: Macmillan, 1964), 68ff.

20. John Milton, *Areopagitica*, in *Complete Prose Works of John Milton;* vol. 2: *1643–1648*, ed. Ernest Sirluck (New Haven: Yale University Press, 1959), 530. A lengthy footnote treats the controversy that has grown up about this statement, although the editor accepts it as an accurate recollection on Milton's part and supports the view that he actually met the aged astronomer on his visit to Tuscany.

21. Cited in William G. Marsden, *From Shadowy Types to Truth: Studies in Milton's Symbolism* (New Haven: Yale University Press, 1968), 127 (my emphasis). Also see E. A. Burtt, *The Metaphysical Foundations of Modern Science* (New York: Anchor Press, n.d.), 75.

22. Bernard Cohen, *The Birth of a New Physics: From Copernicus to Newton* (New York: Anchor Books, 1960), 96.

23. Fletcher, *Intellectual Development*, 356-57.

24. Boyer, *History of Mathematics*, 383.

25. See ibid., 387, for the mathematical process Fermat called "infinite descent."

26. See Derek Thomas Whiteside, "Patterns of Mathematical Thought in the Later Seventeenth Century," *Archive for the History of the Exact Sciences* 1 (1961): 179–388. Another extremely useful study that lays the groundwork for understanding the philosophical notions feeding into seventeenth-century mathematical explorations is Wilbur R. Knorr, "Infinity and Continuity: The Interaction of Mathematics and Philosophy in Antiquity," in *Infinity and Continuity in Ancient and Medieval Thought*, ed. Norman Kretzmann (Ithaca: Cornell University Press, 1982), 112–45. Of particular interest is Knorr's contradictory view regarding the "horror infinitus" attributed to the ancients (142–43).

27. Boyer, *History of Mathematics*, 417.

28. Edna E. Kramer, *The Nature and Growth of Modern Mathematics* (Princeton: Princeton University Press, 1981), 177.

29. See discussion in *Mathematics*, ed. David Bergamini (New York: Time, Inc., 1963), 105. Leibnitz published his version of the calculus before Newton, in 1684; Newton apparently arrived at his version independently, and earlier, but delayed actual publication until 1704.

30. Boyer, *History of Mathematics*, 416.

31. Ibid.

32. See Ernest G. McClain, *The Pythagorean Plato: Prelude to the Song Itself* (Stony Brook, N.Y.: Nicholas Hays, 1978), 128–29. Figure 50 shows the ratios of the ancient Greek modes as recorded by Aristides Quintilianus, and includes the Dorian, Phrygian, Lydian, Mixolydian, Ionian, and Syntolydian modal ratios (155). A particularly useful exposition of the opposition in Aristotelian and Platonic attitudes toward music—and mathematics—may be found in Edward A. Lippman, *Musical Thought in Ancient Greece* (New York: Columbia University Press, 1964); see the chapter entitled "The Peripatetics," esp. 116–17.

33. Arthur E. Barker, "Structural Pattern in Paradise Lost," in *Milton: Modern Essays in Criticism*, ed. Arthur E. Barker (New York: Oxford University Press, 1965), 145.

34. Cited in Cohen, *Birth of a New Physics*, 97, 100. In *Discourses and Demonstrations Concerning Two New Sciences*, Galileo set forth the dynamics of falling objects: "The distances traversed during equal intervals of time by a body falling from rest stand to one another in the same ratio as the odd numbers beginning with unity [1, 3, 5, 7]" and the *spaces* "are to each other as the squares of the time-intervals employed in traversing those distances [1, 4, 9, 16, 25 . . .]." In his description of "uniformly accelerated motion," Galileo failed to take into account the resistance of air.

35. See José A. Benardete, *Infinity: An Essay in Metaphysics* (Oxford: Clarendon Press, 1964), 25–26. Discussing the "Z" (Zeno) series, the mathematical concept of infinite regression, in terms of "limit" and "convergence" from a finitist point of view, Benardete observes, "[H]owever contracted a neighborhood one may choose to envisage surrounding the limiting value 1, we can always generate a *finite* number of terms which lie within the neighborhood . . . greater than any class of terms in the sequence that may be shown to lie outside the neighborhood." I am indebted to the "Scoriae" of Allen Mandelbaum's modern poetic epic, *Chelmaxioms: The Maxims, Axioms, Maxioms of Chelm* (1978), for pointing me to Benardete's invaluable study.

36. Geoffrey Hartmann, "Milton's Counterplot," in Barker, *Milton: Modern Essays in Criticism*, 389. Also see A. S. P. Woodhouse, *The Heavenly Muse: A Preface to Milton* (Toronto: University Press of Toronto, 1972), 215, for a clear account of the mathematical reduction of the demons couched in the form of simile.

37. For Zeno's paradoxes against motion, see chap. 5, note 1.

38. See Benardete, *Infinity*, 72.

39. Røstvig, "The Hidden Sense," 37.

40. A good discussion of the Pythagorean monad can be found in Scott Buchanan, *Poetry and Mathematics* (New York: John Day, 1929), 54–55. This study by a classicist and mathematician is perhaps dated, mathematically speaking, but still one of the most lucid discussions available. See esp. the chapter "Numbers."

41. John Milton, *The Readie and Easie Way to Establish a Free Commonwealth* (2d ed.), in *The Complete Prose Works of John Milton*, vol. 7: *1659–1660*, rev. ed. (New Haven: Yale University Press, 1980), 426. I am grateful to John T. Shawcross for pointing me to Milton's telling analogy here.

42. Kramer, *Modern Mathematics*, 19–20.

43. Benardete, *Infinity*, 41–44.

44. See Paul de Man, "Pascal's Allegory of Persuasion," in *Allegory and Representation: Selected Papers from the English Institute, 1979-80*, ed. Stephen J. Greenblatt (Baltimore: Johns Hopkins University Press, 1981), 1–25. I am indebted to Professor Joshua Wilner for directing my attention to this essay.

45. Ibid., 10.

46. Ibid., 9.

47. I am referring to Fragment 298 of the *Pensées*, discussed at some length

by de Man in "Pascal's Allegory of Persuasion." It should, perhaps, be noted that Erich Auerbach's careful study of the same fragment predates de Man's treatment by thirty years. See Auerbach's essay, "On the Political Theory of Pascal" in *Scenes from the Drama of European Literature*, 101–29. The original German text appeared in *Vier Untersuchen zur Geschichte der französischen Bildung* (Bern, 1951), 51–74. An abridged English version, entitled "The Triumph of Evil in Pascal," was published in *Hudson Review* 4 (spring 1952): 58–79. De Man does not mention the Auerbach study in his own essay, although a number of his observations are in striking conformity with Auerbach's findings.

CHAPTER 4. JAMESIAN GEOMETRY

1. Leon Edel, *Henry James: The Untried Years: 1843–1870* (Philadelphia and New York: J. B. Lippencott, 1953), 301.

2. Henry James, *Italian Hours* (Boston and New York: Houghton Mifflin, 1909), 5. References in the text to *Italian Hours* are to this edition.

3. John Ruskin, *The Stones of Venice: The Foundations* (New York: John Wiley, 1851), app. 8, 379–80.

4. Ibid., sketch XX facing p. 373: "Wall-Veil Decoration" on the Casa Trevisano ("Ca' Trevisan").

5. Edel, *Henry James: The Untried Years*, 301.

6. Ibid., 324.

7. *The Diary of Virginia Woolf*, ed. Anne Olivier Bell, 5 vols. (New York: Harcourt Brace Jovanovich, 1977–1984), 2:136, cited in Daniel Mark Fogel, *Covert Relations: James Joyce, Virginia Woolf, and Henry James* (Charlottesville: University Press of Virginia, 1990). Fogel's meticulously documented study of literary and personal relations, particularly between Woolf and James, has illuminated my own perception of Bloomian "influence," not between the older and younger authors only but also within the plot of *Wings*, as an element to be reckoned with in the characterization of Kate Croy as her father's daughter. Ezra Pound's cranky assessment of *The Wings of the Dove* as "cobwebby" may be found in *Hound & Horn* 7, no. 3 (April–June 1934); the issue is devoted to Henry James.

8. Henry James, preface to *Roderick Hudson*, in *The Art of the Novel: Critical Prefaces by Henry James* (New York: Scribner's, 1953), 5. References in the text to *Art of the Novel* are to this edition.

9. The geometric figures here, one should note, are also figuratively embodied as a stage setting, complete with footlights, or spotlighting.

10. Henry James, *The Wings of the Dove* (1902; reprint, New York: Modern Library, 1909), bk. 6, p. 238. References in the text to *Wings of the Dove* are to this edition.

11. Adeline R. Tintner, *The Museum World of Henry James* (Ann Arbor, Mich.: UMI Research Press, 1986), 96–97.

12. Quentin Anderson has, so to speak, staked out this area in *The American Henry James* (New Brunswick, N.J.: Rutgers University Press, 1957). I do not concur with his approach, which reduces James's late novels to tracts pro-

claiming his father's theological doctrines. Irving Howe bluntly makes the point: "Mr. Anderson, in his passion for abstract system, has betrayed the son by transforming his work into a Swedenborgian 'church' in which the father's insights lay entombed." See Irving Howe, "Henry James as a Latter-Day Saint," in *Celebrations and Attacks: Thirty Years of Literary and Cultural Commentary* (New York: Harcourt, 1979), 78.

13. F. W. Dupee, "Henry James and *The Wings of the Dove*," in *The King of the Cats* (Chicago: University of Chicago Press, 1984), 237.

14. The onomastics are notable, in *Wings*, because the character descriptions afforded by the carefully chosen names points to an allegorical dimension in the novel, while giving information about the characters. For example, Milly Theale not only has Minny Temple's initials, but her name suggests a goddess (in Greek, *thea*) with "millions." Susan Stringham, née Shepherd, suggests a caretaker who is utterly "hamstrung," and Maud Lowder appears both "loud" and "low," or at least "low-born." The names of Lord Mark, and his estate at Matcham will be discussed more comprehensively in the text.

15. Sharon Cameron, *Thinking in Henry James* (Chicago: University of Chicago Press, 1989), 128. Cameron discusses the scene in front of the Bronzino in depth, with sensitivity and insight. One cannot help but be impressed by her meticulous unraveling of the characters' thoughts. Especially persuasive is the proposition that the thought of Milly's resemblance to the woman in the painting "does not arise in her own mind, but rather in Lord Mark's" (129).

16. *The Notebooks of Henry James*, ed. F. O. Matthiessen and Kenneth B. Murdock (New York: Braziller, 1955), 170.

17. I have been greatly helped in reading the geometric symbolism in Henry James, and in other novels of the Victorian and early modern periods, by the sensitivity to iconic structures and the critical intelligence of Felicia Bonaparte's *The Triptych and the Cross: The Central Myths of George Eliot's Poetic Imagination* (New York: NYU Press, 1979).

18. *The Letters of Henry James*, ed. Percy Lubbock (London: Macmillan; New York: Scribner's, 1920), 1:87.

19. Charles Sanders Peirce, "Evolutionary Love," in *Chance, Love, and Logic: Philosophical Essays by the Late Charles S. Peirce*, ed. Morris R. Cohen (1893; reprint, Gloucester, Mass.: Peter Smith, 1949), 268–69. Peirce here glosses Henry James Sr.'s discussion of evil in *Substance and Shadow: An Essay on the Physics of Creation* (1863), in which the elder James argues that "creaturely love" is self-oriented while divine love is other-oriented.

20. Peirce, "Evolutionary Love," 268.

21. For Henry James Sr.'s "vastation," or spiritual crisis, see F. O. Matthiessen, *The James Family: A Group Biography* (New York: Vintage Books, 1980), 6. "James underwent a nervous and spiritual collapse which left him with the conviction of 'the nothingness of selfhood.'" For a more comprehensive account, see R. W. B. Lewis, "Vastation at Windsor, 1844," in *The Jameses: A Family Narrative* (New York: Farrar, Straus & Giroux, 1991), 48–53.

22. Sallie Sears, *The Negative Imagination: Form and Perspective in the Novels of Henry James* (Ithaca: Cornell University Press, 1968), 74.

23. Ibid., 56-7.

24. H. V. Routh, *Towards the Twentieth Century: Essays in the Spiritual History of the Nineteenth* (New York: Macmillan, 1937), 336. This section is entitled "The Edwardian Spirit," and Routh is taking exception to George Moore's assessment of James in *Confessions of a Young Man* (1888). Routh's reading of James as a pragmatist and psychologist, an inventor of hypotheses and solver of problems, provided an apt corrective to the impressionist critiques of the time.

25. Ruskin, *Stones of Venice*, app. 8, 379–80.

26. R. W. B. Lewis, *The Jameses: A Family Narrative* (New York: Farrar, Straus & Giroux, 1991), 522.

27. See Jorge Luis Borges, "The Flower of Coleridge," in *Other Inquisitions, 1937–1952*, trans. Ruth L. C. Simms (New York: Washington Square Press, 1966), 11. Borges explains in a footnote that he has not read James's *The Sense of the Past*, but that he is acquainted with the plot by way of Stephen Spender's analysis of it in *The Destructive Element*.

28. Borges, *Other Inquisitions*, 11.

29. Ibid.

CHAPTER 5. BORGES: "ALGEBRA AND FIRE"

1. Jorge Luis Borges, "An Autobiographical Essay," in *The Aleph and Other Stories, 1933-1969* (New York: Dutton, 1970), 207. Borges refers to Zeno's paradoxes "against motion" repeatedly in his essays and stories. They were originally constructed in support of Parmenides to show the absurdity of pluralist theory. They "prove" you cannot get anywhere. Fleet-footed Achilles can never win the race with the tortoise because the tortoise is given a head start, and Achilles must cover an infinitely diminishing series of spaces before he can run one step. In "Kafka and his Precursors"(1951), Borges sets forth Aristotle's exposition of Zeno's paradoxes: "A moving body A (declares Aristotle) will not be able to reach point B, because before it does, it must cover half the distance between the two, and before that, half of the half, and before that, half of the half of the half, and so on to infinity; the formula of this famous problem is, exactly that of *The Castle*; and the moving body and the arrow and Achilles are the first Kafkian characters in literature." See *Borges, A Reader: A Selection from the Writings of Jorge Luis Borges*, ed. Emir Rodríguez Monegal and Alastair Reid (New York: Dutton, 1981), 242. (References in the text to *Borges, A Reader* are to this edition.) Borges's earlier meditation on Zeno's second paradox, "Avatars of the Tortoise" (1939), traces diachronic variations on the same theme of endless intermediate insertion.

2. See John T. Irwin, *The Mystery to a Solution: Poe, Borges, and the Analytic Detective Story* (Baltimore: Johns Hopkins University Press, 1994). When I completed the first draft of the present chapter, in 1992, the whole thrust of critical analyses of Borges's mathematical bent was centered on his congeniality with Cabala and mystical numerology. Irwin's splendid study goes far beyond the promise of its title, uncovering and apportioning the mathematical, logical,

and rhetorical elements that connect the works of Poe and Borges. Although my own view of the rational or "analytic" elements in the Borges canon coincides with Irwin's, my particular study in this chapter is "The Aleph" (not included in Irwin's category of analytical tales), and my focus is on the specific mathematical concepts that structure that story. I must admit that it is vastly encouraging to find support for my general critical framework in Irwin's beautifully realized and illuminating work.

3. *Alpha-numerical* is the formal term for the combined letter-number system used to classify library holdings. It is worth recalling, in context, that Borges spent many years as a professional librarian: the interchange of letter and number as part of a systematic calculus would have been familiar mnemonic ground for him.

4. See, for example, Jaime Alazraki, "Kabbalistic Traits in Borges' Narration," in *Modern Critical Views: Jorge Luis Borges*, ed. Harold Bloom (New York: Chelsea House, 1986), 79-91. Another serious study is Saul Sosnowski, "'The God's Script'—A Kabbalistic Quest," *Modern Fiction Studies* 19 (autumn 1973): 381–94 (now *MLN*). Robert C. Carroll fully engages Borges's connection with Renaissance hermetic writings in "Borges and Bruno: The Geometry of Infinity in *La Muerte Y La Brújula*," *Modern Language Notes* 94 (1979): 321–42. Borges himself was familiar with Gershom Scholem's *Major Trends in Jewish Mysticism* (New York: Schocken, 1961), and we know from his "Autobiographical Essay" and other sources that Cabala was one of his lecture subjects. See "The Kabbalah" in *Seven Nights*, trans. Eliot Weinberger (New York: New Directions, 1984), 95–106.

5. Emir Rodríguez Monegal and Alastair Reid comment usefully on the "mystical" element in the Borges canon in *Borges, A Reader*, 341-42. They note "his inexhaustible appetite for strange and cryptic lore" but warn that Borges's own disclaimers of belief failed to prevent "solemn Latin American scholars . . . [from] discussing eloquently and at length, B.'s debt to the Cabala." For a persuasive portrait of Borges as pure rationalist, see James E. Irby, introduction to *Other Inquisitions, 1937-1952* (New York: Washington Square Press, 1966). Irby's study "'Tlön, Uqbar, Orbis Tertius'—Borges and the Idea of Utopia" in *The Cardinal Points of Borges* (Norman: Oklahoma University Press, 1971) remains one of the most helpful entries into Borges's modes of thought, including the mathematical.

6. Irby, introduction to *Other Inquisitions*, xii.

7. See *Encyclopaedia Britannica*, 14th ed., s.v. "Kabbalah." A useful work on the history of alphabet and number systems is Karl Menninger, *Number Words and Number Symbols: A Cultural History of Numbers*, trans. Paul Broneer (Cambridge: MIT Press, 1969). A shorter but excellent reference work in this area is Georges Ifrah, *From One to Zero: A Universal History of Numbers*, trans. Lowell Bair (New York: Penguin, 1987). Recently published is the well-researched but more conjectural study by Denise Schmandt-Besserat, *Before Writing: From Counting to Cuneiform*, vol. 1 (Austin: University of Texas Press, 1992).

8. Boyer, *History of Mathematics*, 278.

9. Ibid., 284. Nemorarius is sometimes identified with Jordanus Teutonicus

or Jordanus of Saxony, leader of the Dominican Order, who died in 1237. Howard Eves's *Introduction to the History of Mathematics*, 5th ed. (Philadelphia: Saunders College Publications, 1983), notes that "The Arabic *sifr* was introduced into Germany in the thirteenth century by Nemorarius, as *cifra*, from which we have obtained our present word cipher" (14), and, in a later section, discusses the thirteenth-century mathematician in a passage, chiefly notable for its reversals, that might well have been excerpted from Borges himself: "Next to Fibonacci, and contemporary with him, was Jordanus Nemorarius, usually identified [but in all likelihood mistakenly] with the German monk Jordanus Saxo who, in 1222, was elected the second general of the rapidly expanding Dominican order. He wrote several works dealing with arithmetic, algebra, geometry, astronomy, and [probably] statics. These prolix works, some of which enjoyed considerable fame . . . now seem trivial" (193).

    10. Jorge Luis Borges, "A Vindication of the Cabala," in *Borges, A Reader*, 23.

    11. Borges, "The Kabbalah," 103–4.

    12. Ibid., 99.

    13. Irwin, *Mystery to a Solution*, 83.

    14. Menninger, *Number Words*, 139. Archimedes' *Sand-reckoner* begins with the following argument (in Menninger's translation): "Many people believe, King Gelon, that the grains of sand are without number. Others think that although their number is not without limit, no number can ever be named which will be greater than the number of grains of sand. But I shall try to prove to you that among the numbers which I have named there are those which exceed the number of grains in a heap of sand the size not only of the earth but even of the universe."

    15. Morris Kline, discussing Archimedes' *Sand-reckoner*, gives the procedure: "[Archimedes] takes the largest number then expressed in Greek numerals, that is 10^8, a myriad myriads, and uses it as the starting point of a new series of numbers that goes up to $10^8 \times 10^8$ or 10^{16}. Then he uses 10^{16} as a new starting point for a series of numbers that goes from 10^{16} to 10^{24}, and so forth." See Morris Kline, *Mathematical Thought from Ancient to Modern Times* (New York: Oxford University Press, 1972), 132–33. Kline comments that the importance of Archimedes' work is not as "a practical scheme for actually writing any large number, but the thought that one can construct indefinitely large numbers." This is important in context, for we shall see that Archimedes' procedure in *Sand-reckoner* prefigures Georg Cantor's procedure in constructing the transfinite numbers.

    16. Emir Rodriguez Monegal, Borges's literary biographer, reminds us that "The Library of Babel" was conceived as a nightmare version of the municipal branch library where Borges was employed. He was removed from the position when Perón ("a president whose name I do not want to remember," notes Borges) came into power. See E. R. Monegal, *Jorge Luis Borges: A Literary Biography* (New York: Dutton, 1978) for much good information but a limiting "psychological" slant to the readings. The retired librarian-narrator in "The Book of Sand" is also an echo of Borges the librarian. As in the "Library of Babel," the

parallels between the fictional library and the municipal branch library where Borges worked and wrote are deliberate: "The number of books and shelves were literally what I had at my elbow," Borges affirmed in "An Autobiographical Essay" (Monegal, *Jorge Luis Borges*, 310).

17. Richard Preston, in "The Mountains of Pi," *New Yorker*, 2 March 1992, 38–67, traces the history of the series that originates in the attempt to find the ratio of the circumference of a circle to its diameter (pi = 3.14159265 . . .). Preston quotes mathematician Gregory Chudnovsky's description of pi as "a series of digits that looks like gibberish" (39). Although computers have followed the pi series to a billion places, as of this writing, the digits have never repeated periodically. Preston notes that the number "transcends the power of algebra to display it in its totality."

18. Jorge Luis Borges, "The Book of Sand," in *The Book of Sand*, trans. Norman Thomas di Giovanni (New York: Dutton, 1977), 117. References in the text to "The Book of Sand" are to this edition.

19. Kurd Lasswitz, "The Universal Library," trans. Willy Ley, in *Fantasia Mathematica*, ed. Clifton Fadiman (1901; reprint, New York: Simon & Schuster, 1958), 237–43. This collection contains Willy Ley's helpful "Postscript to 'The Universal Library.'" Borges, in "The Total Library," cites Theodore Wolff's *The Race with the Tortoise* (Berlin, 1929) as a source for the notion of a utopian "total library": "Dr. Theodor Wolff suggests that it is either a derivation from or parody of Raymond Lull's mental machine" (*Borges, A Reader,* 94). Lasswitz and Borges, both, set forth alphanumerical codes found in Wolff.

20. Lasswitz, "Universal Library," 242.

21. Ibid., 243.

22. It should be noted that Borges is conveying historic fact with respect to the mathematical contributions of the Persian poet: see Boyer, *History of Mathematics*, 264-267 and Edna E. Kramer, *Nature and Growth of Modern Mathematics* (Princeton: Princeton University Press, 1981) for the cubic equations Borges is referring to. Kramer says, "Although he used geometric algebra and never arrived at a cubic formula, Omar bin Ibrahim al-Khayyami created techniques of solution for thirteen types of third-degree equation. For this and the applied mathematics by which he devised a calendar superior to our own, Omar is considered to be one of the most original of the Moslem mathematicians. As for the algebra of cubics, his ideas were among the greatest contributions between the fifth and sixteenth centuries (94).

23. Boyer, *History of Mathematics*, 617. Ludwig Wittgenstein commented negatively on Hilbert's remark: "I wouldn't dream of trying to drive anyone out of this paradise. I would try to do something quite different: I would try to show you that it is not a paradise—so that you'll leave of your own accord." See Wittgenstein, *Lectures on the Foundations of Mathematics, Cambridge 1939*, ed. Cora Diamond (Sussex, U.K.: Harvester Press, 1976), 103. Wittgenstein objected to Cantorian sets on the ground that they were as *useful* as Aquinas's angels. In *Remarks on the Foundations of Mathematics* he comments: "I can of course form the expression: 'class of all classes which are equinumerous with the class "infinite series"'" (as also: 'class of all angels that can get on to a needlepoint') but

this expression is empty so long as there is no employment for it." And he concludes, "Such an employment is not: yet to be discovered, but: still to be *invented*" (136).

24. Joseph Warren Dauben, *Georg Cantor: His Mathematics and Philosophy of the Infinite* (Cambridge: Harvard University Press, 1979), 179. This is a superbly lucid study of mid-to-late-nineteenth-century mathematical currents of thought, as well as a carefully documented biography.

25. Boyer, *History of Mathematics*, 615.

26. Dauben, *Georg Cantor*, 69-70. Dauben ascribes the comment on Cantor's counterintuitive theorem to Herbert Meschkowski, a colleague in mathematics.

27. Cited in ibid., 225.

28. Cited in Kramer, *Modern Mathematics*, 577. Einstein is referring to the famous Homeric parody of the *Iliad*, the *Batrachomyomachia* (or "The Battle between the Frogs and the Mice").

29. Jorge Luis Borges, "Baruch Spinoza," trans. Edna Aizenberg, in *Borges and His Successors: The Borgesian Impact on Literature and the Arts*, ed. Edna Aizenberg (Columbia: University of Missouri Press, 1990), 282.

30. Jorge Luis Borges and Adolfo Bioy-Casares, *Chronicles of Bustos Domecq*, trans. Norman Thomas di Giovanni (New York: Dutton, 1976), 67-68.

31. See Umberto Eco, *Semiotics and the Philosophy of Language* (Bloomington: Indiana University Press, 1984), 80-82. The section entitled "The Encyclopedia as Labyrinth" is particularly useful in glossing Borgesian "hypervolumes" and, of course, Eco's own brilliant homage to Borges, *The Name of the Rose*, trans. William Weaver (New York: Harcourt Brace Jovanovich, 1983).

32. Borges and Bioy-Casares, *Chronicles of Bustos Domecq*, 70.

33. Kramer, *Nature and Growth of Modern Mathematics*, 578. For updated conversations between Achilles and the Tortoise, see Douglas Hofstadter, *Gödel, Escher, Bach: A Metaphorical Fugue on Minds & Machines in the Spirit of Lewis Carroll* (New York: Vintage, 1980). A very Borgesian chapter is entitled "Little Harmonic Labyrinth" (103–26). Hofstadter refers directly to Borges's "The Garden of Forking Paths" as an example of Heisenbergian "Uncertainty" in *Metamagical Themas: Questing for the Essence of Mind and Pattern* (New York: Basic Books, 1985), 470, but does not attempt a "reading" of the story.

34. See José A. Benardete, *Infinity: An Essay in Metaphysics* (Oxford: Clarendon Press, 1964), 25–26.

35. As in Kafka's "Metamorphosis," the zero-availability of the sexual object is underscored by the ghost presence of her likeness in a framed photograph.

36. I am using the translation of Norman Thomas di Giovanni, appearing in *The Aleph and Other Stories* (New York: Dutton, 1970), the collection "edited and translated . . . in collaboration with the author," as noted on the title page. Some meanings are changed from the less stylish, perhaps, but more literal translation by Anthony Kerrigan that Borges uses for *A Personal Anthology* (New York: Grove, 1967).

37. See Monegal, *A Literary Biography*, 414–16. Borges had read Dante in the Italian when he worked at the Municipal Library: "A couple of hours each

day, riding back and forth on the tram, I made my way through *The Divine Comedy*, helped as far as the 'Purgatory' by John Aitken Carlyle's prose translation and then ascending the rest of the way on my own" ("An Autobiographical Essay," 242).

38. Jorge Luis Borges, *Labyrinths: Selected Stories and Other Writings*, ed. Donald A. Yates and James E. Irby (New York: New Directions, 1964), 247.

39. Boyer, *History of Mathematics*, 616–17.

40. Dauben, *Georg Cantor*, 182.

41. Ibid., 179.

42. Monegal, *A Literary Biography*, 414.

43. Ibid., 374.

CHAPTER 6. "TEN MINUTES FOR SEVEN LETTERS": *BELOVED*

1. See, for example, Denise Heinz, *The Dilemma of 'Double Consciousness': Toni Morrison's Novels* (Athens: University of Georgia Press, 1993); and Marilyn Sanders Mobley, *Folk Roots and Mythic Wings in Sarah Orne Jewett and Toni Morrison* (Baton Rouge: Louisiana State University Press, 1991); a historic perspective structures Bernard W. Bell's fine essay, "*Beloved*: A Womanist Neo-Slave Narrative; or Multi-vocal Remembrances of Things Past," *African American Review (AAR)* 26, no. 1 (spring 1992): 7–15; while a perceptive analysis of narrative "geometry" can be found in Philip Page's "Circularity in Toni Morrison's *Beloved*," *AAR* 26, no. 1 (spring 1992): 31-39. The psychology of mother-daughter relations is the focus of Jean Wyatt's "'Giving Body to the Word': The Maternal Symbolic in Toni Morrison's *Beloved*," *PMLA* 108, no. 3 (May 1993): 474–88. The mother-daughter relation is also treated in Lillian Corti, "*Medea* and *Beloved*: Self-Definition and Abortive Nurturing in Literary Treatments of the Infanticidal Mother," in *Disorderly Eaters: Texts in Self Empowerment*, ed. Lillian R. Furst and Peter W. Graham (University Park: Pennsylvania State University Press, 1992), 61–67. Finally, the Gothic element is usefully examined by Carol E. Schmudde in "The Haunting of 124," *AAR* 26, no. 3 (fall 1992): 409–16.

2. Margaret Atwood, "Haunted by Their Nightmares," *New York Times Book Review*, 13 September 1987.

3. Walter Clemens, "A Gravestone of Memories," *Newsweek*, 28 September 1987.

4. Philip Page, "Circularity," 36–37. Page cites D. Keith Mano: "As D. Keith Mano points out, the 'allusive, oblique' narrative form enables Morrison to avoid the excessive melodrama that a more straightforward form would have produced" (Mano, "Poignant Instant, Stubborn Evil," review of *Beloved*, by Toni Morrison, *National Review*, 4 December 1987, 55).

5. Toni Morrison, *Beloved* (New York: Penguin, 1988), 270. All subsequent references to this work will appear parenthetically in the text as page numbers following the citation.

6. Ludwig Wittgenstein, *Remarks on the Foundations of Mathematics*

(Cambridge: MIT Press, 1978), 329. In this context, one of the more significant remarks of the later Wittgenstein (1942) has to do with individual perceptions of black and white: "If white turns into black some people say 'Essentially it is still the same'. And others, if the colour becomes one degree darker, say 'It has changed *completely*'." See Ludwig Wittgenstein, *Culture and Value*, ed. G. H. von Wright, trans. Peter Winch (Chicago: University of Chicago Press, 1984), 42ᵉ.

    7. Toni Morrison, "Unspeakable Things Unspoken: The Afro-American Presence in American Literature," *Michigan Quarterly Review* 28, no. 1 (winter 1989): 31.

    8. Ibid., 32.

    9. Ibid., 31.

    10. Ibid., 32.

    11. For a careful study of number in African cultures, see Claudia Zaslavsky, *Africa Counts: Number and Pattern in African Culture* (Boston: Prindle, Weber & Schmidt, 1973). I am indebted to Ray Patterson, poet and colleague, for pointing me to this fine study in sociomathematics. For useful works on number in Western, Indian, Chinese and ancient South American cultures, see Karl Menninger, *Number Words and Number Symbols: A Cultural History of Numbers*, trans. Paul Broneer (Cambridge: MIT Press, 1969); Georges Ifrah, *From One to Zero: A Universal History of Numbers*, trans. Lowell Bair (New York: Penguin, 1987); the more recent study by Denise Schmandt-Besserat, *Before Writing: From Counting to Cuneiform*, vol. 1 (Austin: University of Texas Press, 1992); and Boyer, *History of Mathematics* .

    12. Morrison, "Unspeakable Things Unspoken," 31–32.

    13. Cited in Barbara Offutt Mathieson, "Memory and Mother Love in Morrison's *Beloved*," *American Imago: A Psychoanalytic Journal for Culture, Science and the Arts* 47, no. 1 (spring 1990): 18. This is a rich, lucid reading of the novel, showing a fine discrimination and insight on many levels. Mathieson interprets the "message" of the novel as a personal and social struggle to embrace the past without being controlled by it.

    14. Karla F. C. Holloway, "*Beloved*: A Spiritual," *Callaloo* 13, no. 3 (summer 1990): 516–25.

    15. Charles Dickens, *Hard Times: For These Times* (1854; reprint, New York and Boston: Books Inc., n.d.), 2. Dickens is as much a member of the (white, male) canon as "Aeschylus or William Shakespeare, or James or Twain or Hawthorne, or Melville," all of whom, Morrison states, "I, at least, do not intend to live without" ("Unspeakable Things Unspoken," 5).

    16. Dickens, *Hard Times*, 4. It is, perhaps, of more than incidental interest that *Hard Times* saw first publication in 1854, just one year before Sethe's escape—1855.

    17. Max Black, *A Companion to Wittgenstein's "Tractatus"* (Ithaca: Cornell University Press, 1964), 152.

    18. See Ludwig Wittgenstein, *Tractatus Logico-Philosophicus,* trans. C. K. Ogden (London: Routledge & Kegan Paul, 1922), 188, 189. For Wittgenstein's

comments on knowledge of pain experienced by another, see *The Blue and Brown Books* (New York: Harper, 1960), 48–50.

19. Elizabeth B. House, "Toni Morrison's Ghost: The Beloved Who is Not Beloved," *Studies in American Fiction* 18, no. 1 (spring 1990): 18.

20. I strongly disagree with Corti's treatment of the theme of infanticide in *Medea and Beloved:* "The two works share the same basic plot," she states, and finds that the "banality of child-murder is,perhaps most evident in the world of *Beloved*" (63).

21. See the interview by Melvyn Rothstein, "Morrison Discusses New Novel," *New York Times*, 26 August 1987. I am grateful to my colleague, Professor James Hatch, for pointing out that the Margaret Garner story was part of the source material collected by Morrison in *The Black Book* (New York: Random House, 1974), some thirteen years before the actual publication of *Beloved*.

22. See Bell, "A Womanist Neo-Slave Narrative," 9 n. 1.

23. Holloway, "*Beloved:* A Spiritual," 516.

24. Will Durant, *The Age of Faith: A History of Medieval Civilization—From Constantine to Dante: A.D. 325–1300* (New York: Simon & Schuster, 1950), 390. Information is derived from H. Graetz, *History of the Jews*, trans. Bella Lowy, 6 vols. (Philadelphia, 1891).

25. Toni Morrison, "Black Matter(s)," reprinted in *Falling into Theory: Conflicting Views on Reading Literature*, ed. David H. Richter (1991; reprint, Boston: St. Martin's Press, 1994), 257.

Bibliography

Alazraki, Jaime. "Kabbalistic Traits in Borges' Narration." In *Modern Critical Views: Jorge Luis Borges,* edited by Harold Bloom. New York: Chelsea House, 1986.

Altieri, Charles. *Canons and Consequences: Reflections on the Ethical Force of Imaginative Ideals.* Evanston, Ill.: Northwestern University Press, 1990.

Anderson, Quentin. *The American Henry James.* New Brunswick, N.J.: Rutgers University Press, 1957.

Aristotle. *De motu animalium* (On the movement of animals), translated by A. S. L. Farquharson. In vol. 5 of *The Complete Works of Aristotle,* edited by J. A. Smith and W. D. Ross. Oxford: Clarendon, 1908.

Auerbach, Erich. *Scenes from the Drama of European Literature.* Translated by Ralph Manheim. Gloucester, Mass.: Peter Smith, 1973.

Baker, Henry E. "Benjamin Banneker, the Negro Mathematician and Astronomer." *The Journal of Negro History* 3 (1918): 99–118.

Bakhtin, Mikhail M. *The Dialogic Imagination: Four Essays.* Translated by Michael Holquist and Caryl Emerson. Austin: University of Texas Press, 1981.

Barker, Arthur E. "Structural Pattern in Paradise Lost." In *Milton: Modern Essays in Criticism,* edited by Arthur E. Baker. New York: Oxford University Press, 1965.

Bartley, William Warren. *Wittgenstein.* 2d rev. ed. La Salle, Ill.: Open Court, 1985.

Bell, Bernard W. "*Beloved:* A Womanist Neo-Slave Narrative; or Multi-vocal Remembrance of Things Past." *African American Review* 26, no. 1 (spring 1992): 7–15.

Bell-Villada, Gene H. *Borges and His Fiction: A Guide to His Mind and Art.* Chapel Hill: University of North Carolina Press, 1981.

Benardete, José A. *Infinity: An Essay in Metaphysics.* Oxford: Clarendon, 1964.

Black, Max. *A Companion to Wittgenstein's "Tractatus."* Ithaca: Cornell University Press, 1964.

Blackmur, R. P. *Studies in Henry James.* Edited by Veronica A. Makowsky. New York: New Directions, 1983.

Blake, William. *The Poetry and Prose of William Blake.* Edited David V. Erdman and Harold Bloom. New York: Doubleday, 1965.

Bloom, Harold, ed. *Modern Critical Views: Jorge Luis Borges.* New York: Chelsea House, 1986.

Bonaparte, Felicia. *The Triptych and the Cross: The Central Myths of George Eliot's Poetic Imagination.* New York: New York University Press, 1979.

Borges, Jorge Luis. *The Aleph and Other Stories, 1933–1966.* Translated by Norman Thomas di Giovanni. New York: E. P. Dutton, 1979.

———. *The Book of Sand.* Translated by Norman Thomas di Giovanni. New York: E. P. Dutton, 1977.

———. *Borges, A Reader: A Selection from the Writings of Jorge Luis Borges.* Edited by Emir Rodríguez Monegal and Alastair Reid. New York: E. P. Dutton, 1981.

———. *Ficciones.* Edited by Anthony Kerrigan. New York: Grove Press, 1962.

———. *Labyrinths: Selected Stories and Other Writings.* New York: New Directions, 1964.

———. *Other Inquisitions, 1937–1952.* Translated by Ruth L. C. Simms. Austin: University of Texas Press, 1965. Reprint, New York: Washington Square Press, 1966.

———. *Seven Nights.* Translated by Eliot Weinberger. New York: New Directions, 1984.

Borges, Jorge Luis, with Adolfo Bioy Casares. *Chronicles of Bustos Domecq.* Translated by Norman Thomas di Giovanni. New York: E. P. Dutton, 1979.

Boyer, Carl B. *A History of Mathematics.* Princeton: Princeton University Press, 1985.

Buchanan, Scott. *Poetry and Mathematics.* New York: John Day, 1929.

Burtt, E. A. *The Metaphysical Foundations of Modern Science.* New York: Anchor Press, n.d.

Butler, Christopher. *Number Symbolism.* London: Routledge & Kegan Paul, 1970.

Bush, Douglas. *John Milton: A Sketch of His Life and Writings.* New York: Macmillan, 1964.

Cameron, Sharon. *Thinking in Henry James.* Chicago: University of Chicago Press, 1989.

Carroll, Robert C. "Borges and Bruno: The Geometry of Infinity in *La Muerte y La Brújula.*" *Modern Language Notes* 94 (1979): 321–42.

Cavell, Stanley. *The Claim of Reason: Wittgenstein, Skepticism, Morality, and Tragedy.* Oxford: Clarendon, 1979.

Charney, Maurice. "Hamlet's O-Groans and Textual Criticism." *Renaissance Drama,* n.s., 9 (1978): 109–19.

Cohen, Bernard. *The Birth of a New Physics: From Copernicus to Newton.* New York: Anchor Books, 1960.

Corti, Lillian. "Medea and Beloved: Self-Definition and Abortive Nurturing in Literary Treatments of the Infanticidal Mother." In *Disorderly Eaters: Texts in Self Empowerment*, edited by Lillian R. Furst and Peter W. Graham. University Park: Pennsylvania State University Press, 1992.

Costello, William T. *The Scholastic Curriculum at Early Seventeenth-Century Cambridge*. Cambridge: Harvard University Press, 1958.

Crews, Frederick C. *The Tragedy of Manners: Moral Drama in the Later Novels of Henry James*. New Haven: Yale University Press, 1957.

Dauben, Joseph Warren. *Georg Cantor: His Mathematics and Philosophy of the Infinite*. Cambridge: Harvard University Press, 1979.

de Man, Paul. "Pascal's Allegory of Persuasion." In *Allegory and Representation: Selected Papers from the English Institute, 1979–80*, edited by Stephen J. Greenblatt. Baltimore: Johns Hopkins University Press, 1981.

Devine, Betsy. *Absolute Zero Gravity: A Collection of Jokes, Anecdotes, Limericks, and Riddles, Revealing the Funny Side of Physics, Biology, Mathematics and Other Branches of Science*. New York: Simon & Schuster, 1992.

Dickens, Charles. *Hard Times: For These Times*. 1854. Reprint, New York and Boston: Books Inc., n.d.

Dijkstra, Bram. *The Hieroglyphics of a New Speech: Cubism, Stieglitz, and the Early Poetry of William Carlos Williams*. Princeton: Princeton University Press, 1969.

Dunham, Lowell, and Ivar Trask, eds. *The Cardinal Points of Borges*. Norman: University of Oklahoma Press, 1971.

Dupee, F. W. *Henry James*. American Men of Letters Series. New York: Delta, 1965.

———. "Henry James and *The Wings of the Dove*." In *The King of the Cats*. Chicago: University of Chicago Press, 1984.

Durant, Will. *The Age of Faith: A History of Medieval Civilization—From Constantine to Dante: A.D. 325–1300*. New York: Simon & Schuster, 1950.

Eves, Howard. *Great Moments in Mathematics (Before 1650)*. the Dolciani Mathematical Expositions. Washington, D.C.: The Mathematical Association of America, 1983.

Eco, Umberto. *Semiotics and the Philosophy of Language*. Bloomington: Indiana University Press, 1984.

Edel, Leon. *Henry James: The Untried Years, 1843–1870*. Philadelphia and New York: J. B. Lippincott, 1953.

Elton, William. *King Lear and the Gods*. San Marino, Calif.: Huntington Library, 1968.

Empson, William. *Milton's God*. Rev. ed. London: Chatto & Windus, 1965.

———. *The Structure of Complex Words*. Ann Arbor: UMI Press, 1967.

Engelmann, Paul. *Letters from Ludwig Wittgenstein: with a Memoir*. New York: Horizon Press, 1968.

Fergusson, Francis. "James's Dramatic Form." In *Literary Landmarks: Essays on the Theory and Practice of Literature.* New Brunswick, N.J.: Rutgers University Press, 1975.

Fish, Stanley. *Surprised by Sin: The Reader in "Paradise Lost."* New York: St. Martin's Press, 1967.

Fletcher, Harris Francis. *The Intellectual Development of John Milton.* 2 vols. Urbana: University of Illinois Press, 1956, 1961.

———. *Milton's Rabbinical Readings.* New York: Gordian Press, 1967.

Floyd, Juliet. "The Rule of the Mathematical: Wittgenstein's Later Discussions." Diss., Harvard University, September 1990.

———. "Wittgenstein on 2, 2, 2 . . . : The Opening of Remarks on the Foundations of Mathematics." *Synthese* 87 (1991): 143–80.

Fogel, Daniel Mark. *Covert Relations: James Joyce, Virginia Woolf, and Henry James.* Charlottesville: University Press of Virginia, 1990.

Fowler, Alastair. *Spenser and the Numbers of Time.* Oxford: Routledge & Kegan Paul, 1964.

———. *Triumphal Forms: Structural Patterns in Elizabethan Poetry.* Cambridge: Cambridge University Press, 1970.

Freeman, Eugene, ed. *The Relevance of Charles Peirce.* La Salle, Ill.: Monist Library of Philosophy, 1983.

Frege, Gottlob. "Diary Entries on the Concept of Number." In *Posthumous Writings,* edited by Hans Hermes et al., translated by Peter Long and Roger White. Chicago: University of Chicago Press, 1979.

———. *The Foundations of Arithmetic: A Logico-Mathematical Enquiry into the Concept of Number.* Translated by J. L. Austin. 2d rev. ed. Evanston: Northwestern University Press, 1980.

Freud, Sigmund. "The Antithetical Meanings of Primal Words." In *The Standard Edition of the Complete Psychological Works of Sigmund Freud,* translated by James Strachey, 2:155–61. London: Hogarth Press, 1955.

Furia, Philip, and Martin Roth. "Stevens' Fusky Alphabet." *PMLA* 93, no. 1 (January 1978): 66–77.

Goudge, Thomas A. *The Thought of C. S. Peirce.* New York: Dover, 1950.

Gregerson, Linda. "The Limbs of Truth: Milton's Use of Simile in *Paradise Lost.*" In *Milton Studies XIV.* Pittsburgh: University of Pittsburgh Press, 1980.

Guillen, Michael. *Bridges to Infinity: The Human Side of Mathematics.* London: Rider, 1984.

Hanford, James Holly. *John Milton, Englishman.* New York: Crown, 1949.

Hardy, G. H. *A Mathematician's Apology.* London: Cambridge University Press, 1967.

Hartmann, Geoffrey. "Milton's Counterplot." In *Milton: Modern Essays in Criticism,* edited by Arthur E. Barker. New York: Oxford University Press, 1965.

Heath, Sir Thomas. *A History of Greek Mathematics.* New York: Oxford University Press, 1921.

Heinz, Denise. *The Dilemma of "Double Consciousness": Toni Morrison's Novels.* Athens: University of Georgia Press, 1993.

Heninger, S. K. "Sydney and Milton: The Poet as Maker." In *Milton and the Line of Vision,* edited by Joseph Anthony Wittreich Jr. Madison: University of Wisconsin Press, 1975.

Hofstadter, Douglas. *Gödel, Escher, Bach: A Metaphorical Fugue on Minds and Machines in the Spirit of Lewis Carroll.* New York: Vintage, 1980.

Hofstadter, Douglas R., and Daniel C. Dennet. *The Mind's I: Fantasies and Reflections on Self and Soul.* New York: Basic Books, 1981.

Holloway, Karla F. C. "*Beloved:* A Spiritual" *Callaloo* 13, no. 3 (summer 1990): 516–25.

Hopper, Vincent Foster. *Medieval Number Symbolism: Its Sources, Meaning, and Influence on Thought and Expression.* New York: Columbia University Press, 1938.

Hound and Horn 7, no. 3 (April–May 1934). Special Henry James issue.

House, Elizabeth B. "Toni Morrison's Ghost: The Beloved Who is Not Beloved." *Studies in American Fiction* 18, no. 1 (spring 1990): 17–26.

Howe, Irving. "Henry James as a Latter-Day Saint." In *Celebrations and Attacks: Thirty Years of Literary and Cultural Commentary.* New York: Harcourt, 1979.

Ifrah, Georges. *From One to Zero: A Universal History of Numbers.* Translated by Lowell Bair. New York: Penguin, 1985.

Irby, James E. "'Tlön, Uqbar, Orbis Tertius'—Borges and the Idea of Utopia." In *The Cardinal Points of Borges,* edited by Lowell Dunham and Ivar Trask. Norman: University of Oklahoma Press, 1971.

Irwin, John T. *The Mystery to a Solution: Poe, Borges, and the Analytic Detective Story.* Baltimore: Johns Hopkins University Press, 1994.

James, Henry. *The Art of the Novel: Critical Prefaces by Henry James.* New York: Scribner's, 1953.

———. *Henry James: Autobiography.* Edited by Frederick W. Dupee. New York: Criterion Books, 1956.

———. *Henry James: Selected Literary Criticism.* Edited by Morris Shapira. New York: Horizon Press, 1964.

———. *Italian Hours.* Boston and New York: Houghton Mifflin, 1909.

———. *The Letters of Henry James.* Edited by Percy Lubbock. 2 vols. London: Macmillan; New York: Scribner's, 1920.

———. *The Notebooks of Henry James.* Edited by F. O. Matthiessen and Kenneth B. Murdock. New York: Braziller, 1955.

———. *The Wings of the Dove.* New York: Modern Library, 1909.

James, Henry, Sr. *The Nature of Evil: Considered in a Letter to the Rev. Edward Beecher, D.D. Author of "The Conflict of Ages."* New York: Appleton & Co., 1855.

Janik, Allan, and Stephen Toulmin. *Wittgenstein's Vienna.* New York: Simon & Schuster, 1973.

Johnson, Samuel. *Johnson on Shakespeare*. Edited by Walter Raleigh. London: Oxford University Press, 1965.

Kirk, G. S., and J. E. Raven. *The Presocratic Philosophers*. Cambridge: Cambridge University Press, 1963.

Kittel, Gerhard, ed. *Theological Dictionary of the New Testament*. 12 vols. Grand Rapids, Mich. William B. Eerdman, 1942–67.

Klein, Morris. *Mathematical Thought from Ancient to Modern Times*. New York: Oxford University Press, 1972.

———. *Mathematics and the Search for Knowledge*. New York: Oxford University Press, 1985.

Knorr, Wilbur R. "Infinity and Continuity: The Interaction of Mathematics and Philosophy in Antiquity." In *Infinity and Continuity in Ancient and Medieval Thought*, edited by Norman Kretzman. Ithaca: Cornell University Press, 1982.

Koslov, Arnold. "Ontological and Ideological Issues of the Classical Theory of Space and Time." In *Motion and Time, Space and Matter*, edited by Peter K. Machamer and Robert G. Turnbull. Columbus: Ohio State University Press, 1976.

Kramer, Edna E. *The Main Stream of Mathematics*. New York: Oxford University Press, 1951.

———. *The Nature and Growth of Modern Mathematics*. Princeton: Princeton University Press, 1982.

Kristeller, Paul Oskar. *Facets of the Renaissance*. New York: Harper, 1959.

Lasswitz, Kurd. "The Universal Library." Translated by Willy Ley. In *Fantasia Mathematica*, edited by Clifton Fadiman. New York: Simon & Schuster, 1958.

Lewis, R. W. B. *The Jameses: A Family Narrative*. New York: Farrar, Straus & Giroux, 1991.

Lippman, Edward A. *Musical Thought in Ancient Greece*. New York: Columbia University Press, 1964.

Mallory, William E., and Paul Simson-Housley, eds. *Geography and Literature: A Meeting of the Disciplines*. Syracuse, N.Y.: Syracuse University Press, 1987.

Marsden, William G. *From Shadowy Types to Truth: Studies in Milton's Symbolism*. New Haven: Yale University Press, 1968.

Mathieson, Barbara Offut. "Memory and Mother Love in Morrison's *Beloved*." *American Imago: A Psychoanalytic Journal for Culture, Science and the Arts* 47, no. 1 (spring 1990): 1–19.

Mattheissen, F. O. *Henry James: The Major Phase*. London and New York: Oxford University Press, 1946.

———. *The James Family: A Group Biography*. New York: Vintage Books, 1980.

McClain, Ernest G. *The Pythagorean Plato: Prelude to the Song Itself*. Stony Brook, N.Y.: Nicholas Hays, 1978.

McGuire, J. E., and Martin Tamny. *Certain Philosophical Questions: Newton's Trinity Notebook*. Cambridge: Cambridge University Press, 1983.

Menninger, Karl. *Number Words and Number Symbols: A Cultural History of Numbers*. Translated by Paul Broneer. Cambridge: MIT Press, 1969.

Milton, John. *Areopagitica*. In *Complete Prose Works of John Milton*. Vol. 2, *1643–1648*, edited by Ernest Sirluck. New Haven: Yale University Press, 1959.

———. *Christian Doctrine*. Translated by James Carey. In *Complete Prose Works of John Milton*. Vol. 6, *1658–1660*, edited by Maurice Kelley. New Haven: Yale University Press, 1973.

———. *Paradise Lost*. In *The Complete Poetry of John Milton*, edited by John Shawcross. Rev. ed. New York: Doubleday Anchor, 1971.

———. *The Readie and Easie Way to Establish a Free Commonwealth*. 2d ed. In *The Complete Prose Works of John Milton*. Vol. 7, *1659–1660*, edited by Robert Ayres. Rev. ed. New Haven: Yale University Press, 1980.

Mintz, Samuel I. "The Motion of Thought: Intellectual and Philosophical Backgrounds." In *The Age of Milton: Backgrounds to Seventeenth-Century Literature*, edited by C. A. Patrides and R. B. Waddington. Manchester, U.K.: Manchester University Press, 1980.

Monegal, Emir Rodríguez. *Jorge Luis Borges: A Literary Biography*. New York: E. P. Dutton, 1978.

Monk, Ray. *Ludwig Wittgenstein: The Duty of Genius*. New York: The Free Press, 1990.

Morrison, Toni. *Beloved*. New York: Penguin, 1988.

———. *The Black Book*. New York: Random House, 1974.

———. "Black Matter(s)." In *Falling into Theory: Conflicting Views on Reading Literature*, edited by David H. Richter. Boston: St. Martin's Press, 1994.

———. "Unspeakable Things Unspoken: The Afro-American Presence in American Literature." *Michigan Quarterly Review* 28, no. 1 (winter 1989): 1–34.

Mull, Donald L. *Henry James's "Sublime Economy": Money as Symbolic Center in the Fiction*. Middletown, Conn.: Wesleyan University Press, 1975.

Nicolson, Marjorie Hope. *The Breaking of the Circle: Studies in the Effect of the "New Science" upon Seventeenth-Century Poetry*. Rev. ed. New York: Columbia University Press, 1960.

Ong, Walter J. "Logic and the Epic Muse." In *Achievements of the Left Hand: Essays on the Prose of John Milton*, edited by Michael Lieb and John T. Shawcross. Amherst: University of Massachusetts Press, 1974.

Oppenheimer, Paul. *The Birth of the Modern Mind: Self-Consciousness and the Invention of the Sonnet*. New York: Oxford University Press, 1989.

Page, Philip. "Circularity in Toni Morrison's *Beloved*." *African American Review* 26, no. 1 (spring 1992): 31–39.

Peirce, Charles Sanders. *Chance, Love, and Logic: Philosophical Essays by the Late Charles S. Peirce*. Edited by Morris R. Cohen. Gloucester, Mass.: Peter Smith, 1949.

Perez, Gilberto. "The Narrative Sequence." *Hudson Review* 30, no. 1 (spring 1977): 80–92.

Poulet, Georges. *The Metamorphoses of the Circle.* Baltimore: Johns Hopkins University Press, 1966.

Pound, Ezra. "Henry James." In *Literary Essays of Ezra Pound.* New York: New Directions, 1968.

Preston, Richard. "The Mountains of Pi." *The New Yorker,* 2 March 1992, 38–67.

Rhees, Rush, ed. *Ludwig Wittgenstein: Personal Recollections.* Totowa, N.J.: Rowman & Littlefield, 1981.

Røstvig, Maren Sophie. "The Hidden Sense: Milton and the Neoplatonic Method of Numerical Composition." In *The Hidden Sense and Other Essays.* Norwegian Studies in English, 9. Oslo: Universitetsforlaget; New York: Humanities Press, 1963.

Rothstein, Edward. *Emblems of Mind: The Inner Life of Music and Mathematics.* New York: Random House, 1995.

Rotman, Brian. *Signifying Nothing: The Semiotics of Zero.* New York: St. Martin's Press, 1987.

Routh, H. V. *Towards the Twentieth Century: Essays in the Spiritual History of the Nineteenth.* New York: Macmillan, 1937.

Ruskin, John. *The Stones of Venice: The Foundations.* New York: John Wiley, 1851.

Saunders, Jason. *Greek and Roman Philosophy After Aristotle.* New York: The Free Press, 1966.

Schimmel, Annemarie. *The Mystery of Numbers.* New York: Oxford University Press, 1993.

Schmandt-Besserat, Denise. *Before Writing: From Counting to Cuneiform.* Austin: University of Texas Press, 1992.

Schmudde, Carol E. "The Haunting of 124." *African American Review* 26, no. 3 (fall 1992): 409–16.

Scholem, Gershom. *Jewish Mysticism in the Middle Ages.* New York: Judaica Press, 1964.

———. *Major Trends in Jewish Mysticism.* 3d rev. ed. New York: Schocken Books, 1954.

Sears, Sallie. *The Negative Imagination: Form and Perspective in the Novels of Henry James.* Ithaca: Cornell University Press, 1968.

Shakespeare, William. *King Lear.* Edited by Kenneth Muir. The Arden Edition of the Works of William Shakespeare. London and New York: Methuen, 1972.

———. *"King Lear": Parallel Texts of the First Quarto and the First Folio.* Edited by Wilhelm Vietor. Marburg, 1892.

———. *The Parallel "King Lear," 1608–1623.* Edited by Michael Warren. Berkeley: University of California Press, 1989.

Sheriff, John K. *The Fate of Meaning: Charles Peirce, Structuralism, and Literature.* Princeton: Princeton University Press, 1989.

Sosnowski, Saul. "'The God's Script'—A Kabbalistic Quest." *Modern Fiction Studies* 19 (autumn 1973): 381–94.

Spender, Stephen. *The Destructive Element: A Study of Modern Writers and Beliefs.* London: Jonathan Cape, 1935.

Strehle, Susan. *Fiction in the Quantum Universe.* Chapel Hill: University of North Carolina Press, 1992.

Taylor, Gary, and Michael Warren, eds. *The Division of the Kingdoms: Shakespeare's Two Versions of "King Lear."* Oxford Shakespeare Studies. Oxford: Clarendon; New York: Oxford University Press, 1983.

Tintner, Adeline R. *The Museum World of Henry James.* Ann Arbor, Mich.: UMI Research Press, 1986.

Weiner, Philip P., and Frederick H. Young, eds. *Studies in the Philosophy of C. S. Peirce.* Cambridge: Harvard University Press, 1952.

Williams, William Carlos. *The Collected Poems of William Carlos Williams.* Vol. 1, *1909–1939,* edited by A. Walton Litz and Christopher MacGowan. New York: New Directions, 1986.

Wittkower, Rudolf. *Architectural Principles in the Age of Humanism.* 4th ed. New York: St. Martin's Press, 1988.

Wittreich, Joseph. "'Image of that Horror': History, Prophecy, and Apocalypse in *King Lear.*" San Marino, Calif.: Huntington Library, 1984.

Whaler, James. "The Miltonic Simile." *PMLA* 46 (1931): 1064.

Whiteside, Derek Thomas. "Patterns of Mathematical Thought in the Later Seventeenth Century." *Archive for the History of the Exact Sciences* 1 (1961): 179–388.

Wittgenstein, Ludwig. *The Blue and Brown Books: Preliminary Studies for the "Philosophical Investigations."* Edited by Rush Rhees. New York: Harper, 1960.

———. *Culture and Value.* Edited by G. H. von Wright with Heikki Nyman. Translated by Peter Winch. Chicago: University of Chicago Press, 1984.

———. *On Certainty.* Edited by G. E. M. Anscombe and G. H. von Wright. Translated by Denis Paul and G. E. M. Anscombe. New York: Harper, 1972.

———. *Philosophical Grammar.* Edited by Rush Rhees. Translated by Anthony Kenny. Berkeley: University of California Press, 1978.

———. *Philosophical Investigations.* Edited by G. E. M. Anscombe and R. Rhees. Translated by G. E. M. Anscombe. 2d ed. Oxford: Basil Blackwell, 1967.

———. *Remarks on the Foundations of Mathematics.* Edited by G. H. von Wright, R. Rhees, and G. E. M. Anscombe. Translated by G. E. M. Anscombe. Rev. ed. Cambridge: MIT Press, 1983.

———. *Tractatus Logico-Philosophicus.* Translated by C. K. Ogden. London: Routledge & Kegan Paul, 1981.

Woodhouse, A. S. P. *The Heavenly Muse: A Preface to Milton.* Toronto: University of Toronto Press, 1972.

Wyatt, Jean. "Giving Body to the Word: The Maternal Symbolic in Toni Morrison's *Beloved.*" *PMLA* 108, no. 3 (May 1993): 474–88.

Yates, Frances A. *Giordano Bruno and the Hermetic Tradition.* Chicago: University of Chicago Press, 1964.

Urkowitz, Steven. *Shakespeare's Revision of "King Lear."* Princeton: Princeton University Press, 1980.

Zaslavsky, Claudia. *Africa Counts: Number and Pattern in African Culture.* Boston: Prindle, Weber & Schmidt, 1973.

Index

Algorists, 42–44; and abacist (illustrated), 43

Alphabet: in algebra, 92–93; as classification, 143n. 6; letters as *figurae*, 27–28, 54–55; as names in *Lear*, 37; in *Beloved*, 120; source of number systems, 23–24. *See also* Letter-coding

Anderson, Quentin, *The American Henry James*, 76; 140–41n. 12

Archimedes *(Sand-reckoner)*, 95–96, 97, 99; 144nn. 14 and 15

Aristotle: on Dorian mode, 63; on motion in mathematics, 23

Auerbach, Erich ("Figura"), 26, 55, 130n. 11, 137n. 13; on Pascal, 139–40n. 47

Bakhtin, Mikhail Mikhailovitch *(The Dialogic Imagination)*, 25, 129n. 8

Banneker, Benjamin, 31, 131n. 19

Barker, Arthur E. ("Structural Pattern in *Paradise Lost*"), 63

Benardete, José *(Infinity: An Essay in Metaphysics)*: ambivalence of one and zero, 70; mathematical limit, 68, 139n. 35

Bergson, Henri, 31

Bishop, Elizabeth ("One Art"), 12

Black, Max *(A Companion to Wittgenstein's Tractatus)*: on "linguistic impotence," 124

Borges, Jorge Luis: on Cantor's *Mengenlehre*, 100–102; on Dante, 105, 146–47n. 37; on geometric notion of Godhead, 47; on Henry James, 88–89; interest in numerology, 93–95; mathematical style of, 90–91, 103–4; in pure mathematics, 95; on Spinoza's infinite God, 102. Works: "The Aleph," 21, 24, 91, 103–12; "An Autobiographical Essay," 90; "Baruch Spinoza," 102; "The Book of Sand," 96–97; "The Brotherhood Movement" (with Bioy Casares), 102–3; "The Doctrine of Cycles," 99, 100–102; "The Enigma of Edward Fitzgerald," 98–99; "The Fearful Sphere of Pascal," 47, 135n. 21; "The Flower of Coleridge," 88–89; "The God's Script," 92, 107; "The Kabbalah," 94, 143n. 4; "The Library of Babel," 96; "The South," 107; "Spinoza" (poem), 102; "The Total Library," 96, 97–98; "A Vindication of the Cabala," 93–94

Boyer, Carl B. *(A History of Mathematics)*: "arithmetization" of geometry, 61, 62; on Cantor's

160